W9-ADF-291

If Skies Be Blue

Tell me a story,
If thunder crack,
If rain be falling,
If skies be black.

Tell me a story,
If clouds be few,
If sun be beaming,
If skies be blue.

Tell me a story,
And I'll tell one too—
If skies be cloudy,
If skies be blue.
~Dawn L. Watkins

Reading 2A   Second Edition

 BJU PRESS
Greenville, South Carolina

NOTE:
The fact that materials produced by other publishers may be referred to in this volume does not
constitute an endorsement of the content or theological position of materials produced by such
publishers. Any references and ancillary materials are listed as an aid to the student or the teacher
and in an attempt to maintain the accepted academic standards of the publishing industry.

READING 2-A, Second Edition
If Skies Be Blue

Produced in cooperation with the Bob Jones University
School of Education and Bob Jones Elementary School.

© 1998, 2007 BJU Press
First edition © 1982
Greenville, South Carolina 29614

Printed in the United States of America
All rights reserved

ISBN 978-1-59166-749-0

15 14 13 12 11 10 9 8 7 6 5 4 3 2 1

Contents

Days to Remember

Creatures Great and Small

Treasures

Acknowledgments

A careful effort has been made to trace the ownership of selections included in this textbook in order to secure permission to reprint copyright material and to make full acknowledgment of their use. If any error or omission has occurred, it is purely inadvertent and will be corrected in subsequent editions, provided written notification is made to the publisher.

Houghton Mifflin Company: Glossary material based on the lexical database of the *Children's Dictionary*, copyright © 1981 Houghton Mifflin Company. No part of this book may be reproduced or transmitted in any form or by any means, electronic or mechanical, including photocopying and recording, or by any information storage or retrieval system, except as may be expressly permitted by the 1976 Copyright Act or with prior written permission from both Houghton Mifflin Company and the BJU Press.

"Mice," from *Fifty-One New Nursery Rhymes* by Rose Fyleman. Copyright © 1931, 1932 by Doubleday, a division of Bantam Doubleday Dell Publishing Group, Inc. Used by permission of Doubleday, a division of Bantam Doubleday Dell Publishing Group, Inc. World rights granted by The Society of Authors as the Literary Representative of the Estate of Rose Fyleman.

"This Tooth," from *More Surprises* by Lee Bennett Hopkins. Text copyright © 1987 by Lee Bennett Hopkins. Used by permission of HarperCollins Publishers.

"This Tooth," from *More Surprises* by Lee Bennett Hopkins. Copyright © 1987 by Lee Bennett Hopkins. Reprinted by permission of Curtis Brown, Ltd.

"December Leaves" from *Don't Ever Cross a Crocodile and Other Poems* by Kaye Starbird. Copyright © 1963, 1991 Kaye Starbird. Used by permission of Marian Reiner.

Photo Credits

The following agencies and individuals have furnished materials to meet the photographic needs of this textbook. We wish to express our gratitude to them for their important contribution.

Aramco World Magazine
John Bean
Canine Companions for Independence
Frank Cleland
Creation Science Foundation

Delta Society
Dogs for Disabled
Elm Grove Press
Timm Eubanks
Margo Gathright-Dietrich
Halfmoon Studio

Jon Gnass Photo Images
Breck P. Kent
PhotoDisc, Inc.
Bruce Postle
Frank Turnage
Unusual Films

Kangaroos and Koalas
Creation Science Foundation 109 (all, top by John Bean), 110 (bottom), 111; Photo Disc, Inc. 110 (top); Breck P. Kent 112, 114, 115, 116; Elm Grove Press/Bruce Postle 113

Be Wise About Owls
PhotoDisc, Inc. 157 (both), 158 (top), 159, 160, 162 (bottom); Unusual Films 158 (bottom); Breck P. Kent 161 (both); Frank Cleland/Jon Gnass Photo Images 162 (top)

Service Dogs
Stevie Bunn, courtesy of Dogs for Disabled 173, 177; Unusual Films 174 (all), 175 (middle, bottom); Courtesy of Frank Turnage & Delta Society 175 (top); Linda Ayers Turner Knorr, courtesy of Dogs for Disabled 176 (top); Courtesy of Margo Gathright-Dietrich & Delta Society 176 (middle); photo by Timm Eubanks, Halfmoon Studio, courtesy of Canine Companions for Independence 176 (bottom)

Gold, Frankincense, and Myrrh
PhotoDisc, Inc. 283, 284 (both); Aramco World Magazine, 285 (both); Unusual Films 286

Seth and the Angry Bug

Eileen M. Berry

illustrated by Johanna Berg and Asher Parris

The Dandy Bug

Seth ran to Grandad.

"What's up?" Grandad asked.

"I have to get some bugs for my science project," said Seth. "I must have a box. Can you help me?"

"Yes, I can. I better get one with a lid. Here is a net to help you get the bugs."

Seth spent the next day trapping bugs. He batted his net at a buzzing bumblebee. He ran after a jumpy grasshopper. He hunted a slippery cricket in the sandbox.

3

At the end of the day, he had lots of bugs. He put them in the box with some grass. Then he handed the box to Grandad.

"This one is a dandy," said Grandad.

"What is it?"

"A stinkbug."

"I don't think it smells bad," said Seth.

"Just don't get it mad," Grandad said with a wink. Seth set the box on his bed and ran off to swing.

4

Jenny Bugs Seth

"Grandad! The box is not here! I put it here."
Seth lifted the quilt.

"Stop and think, Seth. It did not go off by
itself," Grandad said.

"Yes, it had to have help," said Seth.

5

"Jenny!" Seth and Grandad ran to her. Seth's little sister Jenny was sitting on the rug. She had the box, and the lid was off!

"Jenny, Seth must have his bugs," said Grandad.

"Bugs not here," said Jenny.

"There is one!" Seth ran to trap the cricket.

"And here is another." Grandad got the grasshopper. But where was the stinkbug?

6

"Sniff a bit, Seth," said Grandad. "I think the stinkbug is mad."

"Jenny, what is that in your hand?"

Jenny held up the stinkbug with a grin. "Bug smelly. It not happy."

"You had better get rid of the stinkbug, Seth," said Grandad. "You can get another bug for the project." Grandad lifted Jenny up.

"Pick happy bug," she said, still grinning. "For Jenny."

7

Sticky Fingers

Stephanie Ralston

illustrated by Paula Cheadle and Johanna Berg

The Jelly Drip

"Bang! Bang!" said Ben. "I got you!" He ran after Randy. A squirrel chattered at them from the big tree.

Randy scampered up the ladder to the tree house. Ben dashed up after him. They stopped to rest.

"I will be the sheriff next time," said Randy. He slid the dishcloth from his chin. It was his robber mask.

Ben nodded. "And I will be the robber, but I'm hungry now." He began to unpack the lunch. Randy bit into his sandwich. A big drop of jelly dripped on the dishcloth.

"You're in for it!" said Ben. "Mom will be upset!"

"I don't think she will! It's just a dishcloth," said Randy. He rubbed the spot with a napkin.

"A dishcloth!" said Ben. "That was a gift from Granny! You better wet it and set it in the sun."

Randy dipped the dishcloth into the water bottle. He put it on a branch to dry.

Ben packed up the rest of the lunch. It was back to the Old West, and the dishcloth with the jelly drip was left to the spring day.

The Scarf

"Have you seen my new scarf?" Mom asked Ben and Randy as they rushed into the kitchen for supper. "Granny comes to visit on Sunday, and I said I would let her see how it looks with my silver pin."

Randy stopped in his tracks.

"You're in for it!" Ben whispered to Randy.

"What are you two up to?" said Dad, coming into the kitchen.

"Randy had it!" said Ben. He looked at Randy. "Randy had Mom's new scarf."

"We were playing. It was a robber mask," said Randy. "It looked like a dishcloth." But he let Ben tell what happened to the dishcloth.

Mom nodded. "That is my scarf. I'm glad you got the jelly off. Would you go get it, Randy?"

"You go with him, Ben," said Dad.

Ben and Randy scampered up the ladder to the tree house. Randy went to the branch to get the scarf. It was missing! A squirrel fussed at them from another branch.

They checked inside the tree house.

They hunted in the grass.

The scarf was not there.

Ben and Randy ran back to the kitchen.

"Did you get it?" asked Dad.

Ben shrugged. "No, it's not on the branch where Randy put it."

"It's missing, Mom!" Randy was upset. "Will you forgive me?"

Mom patted Randy's hand. "Yes, Randy. We will help you hunt," she said.

Mom, Dad, Ben, and Randy hunted after supper, but still the scarf was missing.

At last, they went in. "We will just have to tell Granny," said Mom. "But where could that scarf be?"

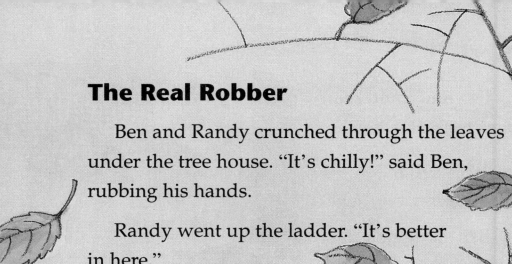

The Real Robber

Ben and Randy crunched through the leaves under the tree house. "It's chilly!" said Ben, rubbing his hands.

Randy went up the ladder. "It's better in here."

Ben went up too.

"We have not played up here since school began!" Ben said. He looked up through the branches. Just a few leaves shivered in the wind.

16

Just then the wind picked up. The top of the big tree bent in the wind.

"What was that?" said Randy, springing up. He grabbed Ben. "What fell from the tree?"

Ben dashed to see what had landed in the leaves. Randy went after him. "I did not see what fell," said Randy.

Ben and Randy sifted through the leaves. Ben held up a tangle of twigs and leaves. "Look, I found a nest!" said Ben.

"I got something too!" said Randy. He held up a cloth. Leaves and little twigs and nut shells stuck to it. "And here's the rest of the nest!"

"That's Mom's scarf!" said Ben. "That is the scarf we played with!"

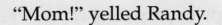

"Mom!" yelled Randy.

"What is it?" asked Mom, running from the kitchen. "My scarf! Where was it?"

"It fell from the tree," said Randy. He patted the big elm.

Ben held up the nest. "This fell with it."

"Well, I never!" said Mom. "A squirrel's nest! What sticky fingers!"

Ben and Randy looked at Mom. "Sticky fingers?" asked Ben.

Mom nodded. "I think a squirrel built its nest with the scarf. It was theft. Someone who robs has sticky fingers. He gets what he wants."

Randy grinned. "Then I was not the real robber," he said. "The squirrel was playing too."

The Tuna Tangle

Dawn L. Watkins

illustrated by Bruce Day

No Lunch Plans

"Where can we get some tuna?" Rags said.

"You can't get the lids off tuna cans," said Jingle.

"We can ask Uncle Mack for help," said Rags.

"He never has tuna. Rags! What is that banging?"

Bump, bump, fiddle, riddle, rumble, tumble, pop!

20

"A rat?" asked Rags. "Want to help me check, Jingle?"

"Me?" said Jingle. "No! I tremble at rats!"

He backed up so fast that he fell off the deck.

Scrap, scrap, rattle, battle, nimble. thimble, plop!

Jingle gasped. "Crabgrass! I will get a rash!"

He sprang up and ran.

Rags ran after his friend.

Jingle smacked into Uncle Mack.

Rags skidded and crashed into Jingle and
Uncle Mack.

**Flap, flap, puddle, muddle, wobble, gobble,
splat!**

"Get up," said Uncle Mack. "You're smashing me!"

Jingle jumped up. He slammed into Rags again, and they went spinning.

Jingle banged into a mop.

"Run!" said Rags.

But the mop dropped on them.

Clink, clink, clatter, splatter, fizzle, drizzle, flop!

Something Fishy

"Stop!" said Uncle Mack. "What is the matter with you?"

"I have crabgrass rash," said Jingle.

"So?" said Uncle Mack. "Can you not just scratch? Must you run into me?"

Rags said, "What is that banging?"

Bump, bump, fiddle, riddle, rumble, tumble, pop!

Uncle Mack said, "Clem has a tuna can."

Jingle said, "Where? We want tuna!"

Jingle stamped into the shed.

"Give us that tuna!" Jingle said.

He thumped Clem.

Clem just blinked.

"You tremble at rats," said Rags. "But you hit dogs?"

"No one gets my tuna!" said Jingle.

"Just me," said Uncle Mack. He put the tuna can into his vest. "Clem gets the lids off for me. Coming, Clem? Tuna for lunch!"

Rags said, "You! I will thrash you into tuna hash!"

"If you can catch me," said Jingle.

Zip, zip, scramble, ramble, frizzy, dizzy, zap!

Someone My Age

Milly Howard / illustrated by Sherry Neidigh

Tessa Wants a Friend

"May I go jump rope, Mother?" asked Cassy.

Mother smiled. "Yes," she said.

"May I ride my bike?" asked Kent.

"Yes," said Mother.

Tessa went to sit on the steps. Mother came to sit with her.

"Mother," Tessa said, "Cassy has a friend in Apartment 28. Kent has a friend in Apartment 32. But I don't have a friend here."

"You have friends at school," said Mother. "You can ask one of them to come home with you."

"That is not the same as having a friend who lives close to me," said Tessa.

"Well," Mother said. "The Blakes are renting Apartment 48. I met them when they came to look at the apartment. They had someone your age with them. Maybe she will be your friend."

Tessa looked up and smiled. Mother gave her a hug. "Why not skate awhile," she said.

Tessa ran to get her skates. Mother helped her put them on. Off Tessa skated. She waved at Cassy and her friend. They were skipping rope.

Kent and his friend were riding bikes. Tessa waved as they rode past her.

Someone Tessa's Age

Tessa skated back to her apartment. A van drove up to the apartments and stopped. Tessa stopped to look. The van backed up to Apartment 48!

Tessa skated a little closer. She could see a man and a lady taking in a little table. She could see them taking in plants and a cooler. She could see them taking in one box after another. When the man lifted a bike from the back of the van, Tessa skated even closer to look. "It's a bike just like mine!"

The lady looked up. "Hello," she said. "I am Mrs. Blake. Who are you?"

"I am Tessa Stevens," Tessa said. "I am seven. Do you have someone my age?"

The lady smiled. "Yes, Simone is helping. Come here, Simone," she said.

Simone came through the door. She stopped and looked at Tessa.

"Hello," said Tessa.

Simone just smiled. Then she went back inside Apartment 48.

→ "Simone is shy," said her mother. "Just give her more time. She would like to have a friend. Come back and visit us."

"I will," said Tessa. She skated home.

One Step, Two Steps

When Tessa got home, Mother was fixing dinner.

"Did you see someone your age?" asked Mother.

Tessa dropped her skates in the box. "Yes," she said. "I spoke to her, but she did not speak to me."

"Did she hear you?" asked Mother.

"Yes," Tessa said. "But she is shy."

"Why not try speaking to her every day? You can ask her to go with you to Sunday school," Mother said.

And that is what Tessa did.

Every day she skated past Apartment 48. Every day she spoke to Simone.

"Would you like to go to Sunday school with me?" she would ask.

"No, thank you," Simone would reply.

One day Simone was sitting on her steps. She had some skates in her hand.

Tessa stopped. "Can you skate?" she asked.

"Not yet," said Simone.

"You just take one step, then two steps and slide," said Tessa. "Let me help."

She helped Simone put on her skates. Then Tessa skated beside Simone. Simone wobbled from side to side. At last she stopped to rest.

"Do you still go to Sunday school?" asked Simone.

"Yes," said Tessa. "Will you go with me?"

"Mother said that I could go. Will you stop for me Sunday?" Simone asked.

"Yes, I will," Tessa said with a smile.

Tessa hummed as she skated home. "Thank you, Lord," Tessa said. "You gave me a friend close by, someone who is just my age!"

Little Bug's Trip

Becky Davis and Jan Joss
illustrated by Stephanie True

Little Bug Leaves Home

Little Bug bent over and looked at himself in the lake. He fixed his little red cap just so.

"I am quick. I am brave. I am clever. I am the best bug there is," he said.

His chest swelled until a button popped from his crisp red coat.

"It is time for me to leave home. I can take care of myself," Little Bug said.

Little Bug tilted his little bug cap, tied his little bug shoes, and checked the other two buttons on his little bug coat. Then he buzzed away.

He hummed happily to himself as he left. "I am quick. I am brave. I am clever. I am the best, and that is that."

Little Bug landed on a rock. A duck was coming by.

"Quack, quack," he heard the duck say. She opened her beak, flapped her wings, and said, "Come play with me and be my friend, Little Bug."

"Oh, ho!" Little Bug bragged to himself. "This duck would like to see what a fine bug I am."

He buzzed closer and sat on a red and yellow leaf.

"You are a *fat* bug!" quacked the duck, nodding. "I like fat bugs the best."

Little Bug tipped his little bug cap. He began to speak. But before he could say anything— snap! went the duck's yellow bill.

The duck got Little Bug's shoe. A sudden breeze sent the red and yellow leaf flying. Little Bug was safe underneath the leaf, but his little legs were shaking!

Little Bug Hides

Little Bug peeked up from underneath the leaf. He could not see or hear the duck anywhere.

"Oh, oh!" he said to himself. "That duck was quick!"

Little Bug wiggled from under the leaf. One of his two little bug shoes was missing. Another button was gone from his little bug coat. But his little bug cap was still in place.

"I am not quick. But I am brave, and I am clever," he said.

Little Bug puffed up his chest so big that the last button popped from his little bug coat.

Suddenly, a black shadow fell over him. Little Bug heard a flap, flap. He looked up. A big black crow was flying closer and closer to him!

Little Bug could feel himself shaking. He was shaking from the top of his little bug antennae to the tips of his little bug toes.

He ran back to hide under the leaf. His little legs were shaking, and his little wings were quivering!

The black crow flapped his wings and went away. Little Bug's teeth stopped chattering. He buzzed away and landed on a rose.

Little Bug tapped the brim of his little red cap. He said, "I am not quick and I am not brave, but I am clever."

He buzzed closer to the lake.

Little Bug Buzzes Home

"I see a frog," Little Bug said to himself. "I am more clever than he is."

"Is that a bug?" croaked the frog, hopping onto a lily pad. "Come closer, Little Bug. Give me a better look at you. I would like to see what a fine bug you are."

Little Bug sat on a stick closer to the frog. But the frog said, "I have lived many years and cannot see well. Come closer still."

43

Little Bug buzzed to the end of the stick.
"I am a fine-looking bug, friend Frog," he said.
But before he could say anything else—zap!
went the old frog's tongue.

But the frog just got the little red cap.

Splash! Little Bug's last shoe fell into the lake. His open coat flapped as he buzzed quickly to a treetop.

"That frog was clever!" he said. "If he could see well, I would not be here!"

Little Bug sat to think. "I am not quick. I am not brave. I am not clever. I can see my side of the lake. I am going home."

And he did.

Samuel, God's Servant

(based on I Samuel 2–3)

Becky Davis
illustrated by Del Thompson

In the Tabernacle

One day Samuel's mother went with him to the tabernacle. "Beginning today you will live in the tabernacle with Eli," she said. "You can serve God here."

Samuel asked, "Will you visit me?"

"Yes, I will visit you every spring," said his mother.

Samuel's mother hugged him and kissed him. She was very sad, but she left him in the tabernacle with Eli.

"I am glad you have come, Samuel," said Eli. "I cannot do some of the jobs here. You will be a big help."

Samuel was happy in the tabernacle. He lit the lamps. He rubbed the brass cups with a rag. He ran here and there to get things for Eli.

Samuel was a servant of God.

Who Was Speaking?

Eli's sons did not serve God. Their sins before the Lord were very great. But Eli did not punish his sons. He let them live in God's tabernacle.

God was not happy with Eli's sons. He was not happy with Eli. But God could see that Samuel wanted to serve Him. God could speak to Samuel.

One day after Samuel had finished his jobs, he went to bed. Suddenly, in the stillness, Samuel heard someone speak to him!

"Samuel! Samuel!" someone said.

Samuel jumped up from his bed and ran to Eli. "Here I am, Eli. Did you want me?"

Eli blinked and looked at Samuel. "I did not speak to you," Eli said. "Go back to bed."

Samuel went back to bed. But he did not understand. "Someone was speaking to me," he said to himself. "Who was it?"

"Samuel!"

Samuel jumped up from his bed and ran back to Eli. "Here I am, Eli," he said. "You did want me."

"No, I did not want you," Eli said. "Go back to bed."

Samuel went back to bed. But he could not rest.

God's Servant

"Samuel!"

Samuel rushed back to Eli. "I heard you, Eli! I did hear you speak! You wanted me!"

Eli sat up on his bed. He did not tell Samuel to go back to bed. Eli said, "Samuel, maybe God was speaking to you. Next time you must answer. Say, 'Speak, Lord, for Your servant hears.' "

Back in bed, Samuel lay awake. Everything was still until he heard someone speak.

"Samuel!"

Samuel's chin trembled. But he remembered what Eli had said to do. He answered, "Speak, for Your servant hears."

God said, "Samuel, Eli's sons are wicked. Eli has not punished them. So I must punish Eli and his sons. They have not served Me."

The next day Eli said, "Samuel, what did God tell you?"

Samuel did not want to tell Eli what God had said. But he did tell him. Eli nodded. "The Lord will do what is best," he said.

God kept on speaking to Samuel when he was a lad and after he was a man. Samuel would tell everyone what God said. He was the servant God wanted.

BILLY SUNDAY

Karen Wilt / illustrated by Del Thompson

A Baseball Player Gets Saved

The streetcar ran clicking and clacking on its rails. Anne sat by her father, humming the tune they had sung at the tent meeting. "Papa," she said at last, "I liked hearing Mr. Sunday preach. Did you ever see him play baseball?"

"Yes, Anne," Father said. "I saw him play before he began preaching in tent meetings. Mr. Sunday ran like the wind when he played baseball. Because he could run so fast, he could catch more fly balls than any of the other players."

The wind came through the streetcar's open glass window, brushing Anne's face. "I wish I had seen him," Anne said.

"Mr. Sunday helped his team, the White Stockings, win lots of games," Father said. "There it is, Anne." He was looking through the window. "There's the church where it happened."

"What happened, Papa?" Anne waited for Father's story.

"One day Mr. Sunday was walking with two of the men on his baseball team. They heard singing. It made Mr. Sunday think of his mother's singing. His friends went home, but Mr. Sunday stayed to listen.

"A man preached. He said that Christ had come to save sinners. Mr. Sunday left, but he did not forget what the preacher had said. One glad day, Mr. Sunday asked Christ to take away his sins and save him."

"He trusted Christ, just like I did today!" Anne exclaimed.

"Yes, Anne." Father gave her a hug.

A Long Reach

· The streetcar brakes screeched to a stop. Another passenger climbed onboard. "What did Mr. Sunday do after he was saved?" Anne asked. She sat closer to Father. She wanted to hear more.

"Mr. Sunday kept playing baseball. One day his team played a big game. The game was really close. The best man on the other team was up to bat.

"The White Stockings waited for their pitcher to toss the ball. Just as he let it go, his leg slipped. The ball went where the batter wanted it. The batter hit that ball with a crack! It went flying across the ballpark. Mr. Sunday began to run. This was not the time to miss. He had to catch that ball or the game would be lost!"

The streetcar's clicks and clacks got closer together. The wheels spun faster and faster.

"Mr. Sunday ran as fast as he could. He wanted his team to win. He had to catch that ball. 'Lord,' he prayed, 'help me to catch that ball!' Mr. Sunday ran to the end of the ballpark. His eyes never left that ball. He saw the ball starting to fall. He held up his mitt and jumped."

"He prayed to catch the ball?" Anne asked.

"Yes, and the ball hit his mitt with a thump, but Mr. Sunday kept going. He tripped over a bench and fell under some horses. When he picked himself up, the ball was still in his mitt!

"Everyone yelled and yelled. Billy Sunday's team had not lost the game! The White Stockings were the winners."

God's Preacher

Electricity crackled as the long rod on top of the streetcar hit the wires over the street. "Why did Mr. Sunday stop playing baseball, Papa?" Anne asked.

"God had a plan for Mr. Sunday, Anne," Father said, "just as He has a plan for you and every other Christian. God's plan for Mr. Sunday was for him to be a preacher. Mr. Sunday wanted to do what God wanted, but he liked playing baseball too.

"One day he said, 'I will quit playing baseball if my team will let me go. I said I would play for them for three years. I cannot leave if they will not let me.'

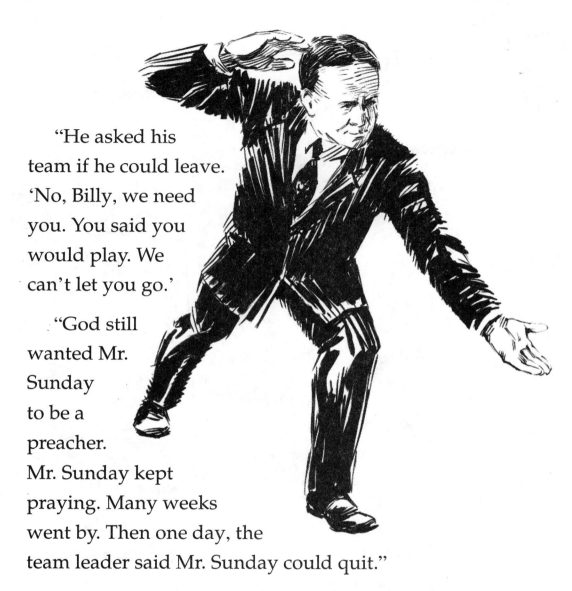

"He asked his team if he could leave. 'No, Billy, we need you. You said you would play. We can't let you go.'

"God still wanted Mr. Sunday to be a preacher. Mr. Sunday kept praying. Many weeks went by. Then one day, the team leader said Mr. Sunday could quit."

"God answered him," Anne said.

"Yes, God answered, so Billy Sunday became a preacher for Christ."

The streetcar stopped at the end of their block. Father and Anne got off, and the streetcar click-clacked away.

"Mama!" Anne called when they reached the steps. "We heard Mr. Sunday preach today in the tent meeting. He was a baseball player before he became a preacher. Papa saw him play one time. And Mama, today at the tent meeting I asked Christ to save me!"

Mother gave Anne a kiss. "Good! I am glad," she said. "God has a plan for your life, Anne."

"Yes, just like He had a plan for Mr. Sunday," Anne said. "God heard him, and He heard me too."

This Tooth

Lee Bennett Hopkins / illustrated by Johanna Berg

I jiggled it
jaggled it
jerked it.
I pushed
and pulled
and poked it.

But—
As soon as I stopped, and left it alone,
This tooth came out on its very own.

To Market

Susan W. Young / illustrated by Sherry Neidigh

Over the River

"It will soon be spring," said Hildy to Fritz. "You must go to market and buy some corn to plant."

"I will go to market and buy some corn," said Fritz. "I will buy a big, fat goose too. We will have a feast for our friends, and then I will plant the corn."

In the morning Fritz set off for the market. He had to go over the river. He would use his little boat.

It was noon when Fritz got to the market. First, he bought a fat goose for the feast. He put the goose under his arm and went to buy a bag of corn.

He got the corn. Then he put the bag of corn on his back and the goose under his arm.

It was time to go home. He must hurry back to the river.

But along the way Fritz saw a man with a fine, red fox. "I will buy this fine, red fox and give him to my wife," said Fritz. "He will make a good pet."

He put the goose under his arm and the bag of corn on his back. The fox followed him on a rope.

Fritz was very tired when he got to the river. He stopped to rest. He looked at his little boat. He looked at the goose. He looked at the fox. Fritz was not happy. The boat was too small, and they would not all fit.

"We must get over the river," said Fritz.

And Back Again

"What a predicament!" Fritz thought. He could not leave the fox with the goose. The fox would eat the goose. He could not leave the goose with the corn. The goose would eat the corn.

He had to go over the river soon, or it would be too dark to see the way home.

"I will take the goose first!" he said. "I can
leave the fox with the corn. He will not eat the
corn." Fritz took the goose to the other side. He
put the goose under a big tree on the bank.

Fritz went back to get
the corn. He took the corn to
the other bank and put it under
the tree. But he could not leave the
corn with the goose.

"The goose will eat the corn,"
he said. He sat under the tree.
He thought and thought.
He looked at the goose.
He looked at the corn,
and he looked at the boat.

"I have a plan. I will leave
the corn under the tree and take
the goose back to the other
side." He put the goose in the
boat and went back over the
river to get the fox.

71

He stopped the boat at the bank. He put the
goose on the bank and put the fox in the boat.
It was getting late. He had to hurry.

He went over the river to the tree. He put the
fox under the tree with the corn.

"The fox will not eat any corn," he said. "So
I will get the goose, and then I can go home."

Fritz went back to get the goose. When he
got back to the tree, he put the bag of corn on
his back and the goose under his arm. The fox
on the rope followed him home. He was not too
late. The sky was not dark. He could see the
way home.

A Promise to Remember

Dawn L. Watkins and Eileen M. Berry
illustrated by John Roberts

Cast

Mr. Allerton

Mrs. Allerton

Remember Allerton

Mr. Mullins

Mrs. Mullins

Joseph Mullins

Sailor 1

Sailor 2

Four friends
of Sailor 1

Act I

(Mr. and Mrs. Allerton and Mr. and Mrs. Mullins are sitting at a table. Remember and Joseph are playing in a corner.)

Mr. Allerton: We have to choose. The king has said we must go to his church. But we cannot go there and be true to our God.

Mr. Mullins: We can choose to obey the king. Or we can choose to obey God.

Mrs. Allerton: It seems that there is just one thing to do.

Mrs. Mullins: That's true. We must do what God says. But we cannot stay here if we choose God's way.

Mrs. Allerton: Then it is settled? We will leave this land?

Mr. Allerton: Yes, we must sail to a new land— America.

Mrs. Mullins: It will be hard to leave the friends we have met in this land.

Mrs. Allerton: Yes. And there is much to do. We will have to pack the things we will need in the new land.

Mr. Mullins: We must remember that God will take care of us. He will go with us.

Remember *(to Joseph)*: I wish we could stay.

Joseph: Why? It will be fun to ride on the *Mayflower*. Maybe we can even get out and ride in small boats sometimes.

Remember: I don't like small boats. They rock too much.

Joseph: We'll have lots of room to play in the new land. There will be no one there but us.

Remember: Mother says there will be Indians. I am afraid.

Joseph: The Indians will be our friends. We'll play with them. Just wait and see.

Mrs. Allerton: Come, Remember. Shall we think about what to pack?

(Remember stands up and goes to the table.)

Mr. Allerton: One thing you won't need to take is your fear. Our God says, "I will never leave thee." Remember that.

Act II

(Remember and Mr. and Mrs. Allerton are standing at the rail of the ship. Sailor 1 is sitting off to one side of them, twisting some ropes.)

Remember: How much longer will we be on the *Mayflower*, Father?

Mr. Allerton: Many more days, Remember.

Sailor 1 *(mocking):* Yes, many more days to be sick. Many more days to smell of fish and tar. Many more days for me to hear your silly stories of your God.

Mr. Allerton: We hope to reach America soon, sir. Then you will be rid of us.

Sailor 1: Ha, ha! That is true. Those of you who make it to America will soon die there. You will be tired and hungry. It is too hard for you to live in a new land.

Remember (*whispering to Mr. Allerton*): I wish that man would not make fun of us.

Mr. Allerton: It does not matter what he says. Remember what God says? "I will never leave thee." He is still with us.

Mrs. Allerton: Let's go to bed and get some rest.

(Mr. and Mrs. Allerton lie down. Sailor 1 leaves the stage.)

Remember *(kneeling):* God, please don't let us die like that man said. I am so afraid. Please take care of us.

(Remember lies down.
Just before dawn,
Joseph comes and
shakes her.)

Joseph: Wake up, Remember! The sailors are
  going to throw a man off the ship.

Remember *(rubbing eyes)*: Why?

Joseph: He got sick and died.

(Remember and Joseph watch four friends of Sailor 1 pass by, dragging Sailor 1 on a blanket.)

Remember *(whispering)***:**
Joseph! That's the sailor who made fun of us! He said we were all going to die.

Joseph: Yes. And now he is the one who died.

Remember: I think God is going to take care of us.

Joseph: I do too! Let's tell the others.

Act III

(Remember and Mrs. Allerton are sitting on deck.)

Remember: I feel so tired. So many are sick—
even Joseph.

Mrs. Allerton: Yes. It has been a hard trip.

Remember: What if we never see land again?
I don't want to die on this ship.

(Remember starts to cry softly. Mrs. Allerton hugs her gently.)

Mrs. Allerton: Let me tell you why your father and I named you Remember. We wanted you to remember that God is good. We wanted you to remember that He loves you and wants to help you. We wanted you to remember all of the things He has promised in the Bible.

Remember: Like "I will never leave thee"?

Mrs. Allerton: Yes, promises just like that one.

Remember (*still sniffling, but nodding*): I will try to remember.

(Mrs. Allerton leaves. Mrs. Mullins comes to Remember.)

Mrs. Mullins: Remember! Here you are.

Remember: How is Joseph, Mrs. Mullins?

Mrs. Mullins: He is not very well. He wanted you to come and see him.

(Remember and Mrs. Mullins go to Joseph, who is lying on a blanket. Remember kneels.)

Remember: I hope you are better soon, Joseph. I miss our games.

Joseph: Mother, do you think I'll get better?

Mrs. Mullins: I think so, Joseph. You need rest. If we can just reach land soon . . .

Remember: Don't be afraid, Joseph. Think about God. Remember, He will never leave you.

(In a corner, Sailor 2 steps up on a stool and shades his eyes with his hand.)

Sailor 2 *(very excitedly)*: Land ho!

(All Allertons and Mullinses run to the rail. Joseph stands up and walks slowly to join them.)

Mr. Mullins *(pointing)*:
There it is! America, our new home.

(All clap and cheer.)

Mr. Allerton:
God keeps His promises. This is a day to remember.

Creatures Great and Small

Philip and His Farm

Stephanie Ralston

illustrated by
Ruth Ann Ventrello

Pet Problems

Cats, dogs, hamsters—
Achoo! Just the names make
me sneeze! Pardon me, sniff
sniff, but I have allergies.

Oh, my name is Philip.
Did I tell you that yet?
Anyway, you know the
tickle in your nose that
you get when you need
to sneeze? Well, pets make
my nose tickle. And pets
make me sneeze.

Knows
nose

Do you know how hard that is? It started
with Cat. I sneezed, sneezed, sneezed. So Cat
left, and then we got Dog—Dog had short fur.
Still, it was sneeze, sneeze, sneeze. So Dog left.
And then we got Hamster. Then it was just
sneeze, sneeze. A little better, but still the tickle!
Then Hamster left. So Mom said, "That's it!
We must try something new."

And that's how we got Crabcake.

Crabcake was a hermit crab. At first, I called him Hermit, but my big brother Josh said that Hermit was a silly name. So Josh started calling him Crabcake, and the name stuck.

Stud

At first, I was excited to have Crabcake. I watched him every day after school. But in a week or so, I started to think that crabs were dull. boring Crabcake didn't do anything but sit. Oh, he would crawl, but he was so slow! And seeing him stuck inside that shell every day made me just want to run away and play. I didn't sneeze much, but I didn't really like Crabcake—at least, not as a pet owner should like his pet.

Soon Crabcake left, but I was only sad because I didn't have a pet anymore.

Then Granny came to visit.

Granny Decides

"A fish?" said Granny.

stick

I shook my head. "My friend has a fish, and it stinks."

"A toad?" said Granny.

I shook my head. "Warts."

Granny said, "Toads don't give warts."

But I still didn't want to risk it.

"A lizard?" said Granny.

I started to think on that one, but Mom said, "No, that is where I draw the line."

"Good," said Granny. I looked at her. She
was happy that I didn't want any of those pets!

Granny went to her room and came back
with gloves, a big glass jar, a plastic bag, and
a shovel.

"We're going to make an ant farm," she said
and marched into the yard.

I followed her, but I didn't think an ant farm would be that great. Still, she might need my help.

Granny put some ants in a bag and some ants in the soil in the jar. "We must do this with care," she said. "There! That should do."

She marched inside the house. I followed her. I still didn't see how this ant farm would work.

Later that night, Granny showed me the ants. She had put them all in the jar.

"See those ants?" said Granny. She was watching some of the ants dig a tunnel. "Those are the workers. Those bigger ones are soldiers. Those little white things are eggs. And that big one is the queen. You watch them for the next week or two. This will soon be a neat, smoothly run colony."

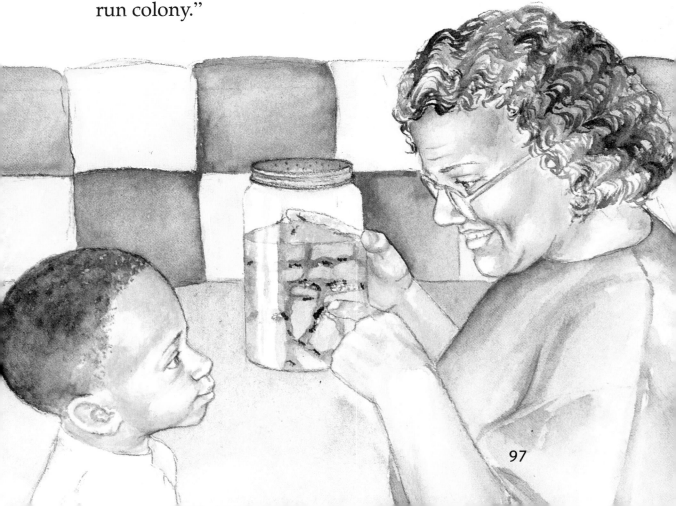

The next few weeks, I fed the ants honey and water every two days. Granny was right! Boy, those ants were busy! Every time I saw them, I wanted to be busy too. And you know what? I didn't even sneeze.

My First Lamb

When my first lamb was born,
Frost lay under feet;
He would not eat, my lamb,
But only bleat and bleat.

When my first lamb was born,
I called him Simon James;
"If he won't eat," said Pa,
"No need to give him names."

When my first lamb was born,
I sat there in the hay;
I stroked his thick curled wool
And cooed him all the day.

When my first lamb was born,
I prayed that God would hear;
And when the sun went down,
Lamb let the ewe come near.

When my first lamb was born,
I thanked the Lord with tears;
"You named him well," Pa said,
"For Simon means 'He hears.' "

Dawn L. Watkins

illustrated by
Johanna Berg

99

Little Lost Lamb (taken from Luke 15:4-7)

Karen Wooster / illustrated by Bob Martin and Johanna Berg

All but One

"Come, my flock," the shepherd called. "It is time to go home. It will be night before we get to the fold."

The shepherd led the way home. The sheep trusted him and followed closely. The little lambs ran by their mothers' sides. Puffs of dust filled the air as the many tiny feet trotted along the path.

All the sheep followed the shepherd—all but one.

One little lamb stopped to nibble on a clump of grass. Then he saw some greener clumps of grass a little farther away. The little lamb left the path to eat some of the good green grass. He nibbled another clump and then another. He heard the other sheep going home, but he kept straying farther and farther away.

The rest of the flock trotted over the hill back to where they lived. The little lamb was all alone.

One Is Missing

"Sixty-one, sixty-two, sixty-three," the shepherd said as he counted the sheep. The sheep trotted past him into the fold.

The shepherd and his sheep were safe at home. Here the strong stone wall would keep the flock until morning. Here the robbers could not steal the flock. Here the animals could not kill the sheep.

The shepherd counted the last of the flock. "Ninety-seven, ninety-eight, ninety-nine." There were no more sheep to go into the fold.

"One lamb is missing," said the shepherd. "Where could he be? Maybe his leg is cut. Or robbers may have tried to steal him. An animal may even have snatched him away.

"I must go look for the lost lamb!" he said. The shepherd's heart was broken because he loved each of the lambs.

As the shepherd left to look for the lamb, the sky became dark. The ninety-nine sheep were safe in the fold. One stray lamb was not.

Storm clouds were filling the sky now. Far away the thunder rumbled. The wind began to blow very hard. Still the shepherd looked. He could not see the little lost lamb anywhere.

The shepherd called out to the lamb and then listened for the lamb's cry.

By now raindrops were pounding on the ground. Drawing his cloak closer, the wet shepherd struggled along.

Somewhere out in the storm was a little lost lamb.

"Baa, baa." The shepherd heard the faint cries from far away.

"That must be my stray lamb," said the shepherd.

The shepherd left the path. He climbed over the rocks. Still he could not find the lamb.

Found

The shepherd looked
down the side of a steep cliff.
There caught on a rock below
was the little lamb. The frightened
lamb lay by the side of the cliff. Just
one more step and the lamb would fall.

The shepherd lowered his staff and lifted
the lamb up.

The little lamb's fluffy white coat was now tattered and torn. Thorns had ripped his soft fluff.

"I'm glad the wild beasts did not find you before I did," said the shepherd.

With the lamb in his arms, the shepherd started home. The storm had passed.

When they were safe at home, the kind shepherd began to clean the bleeding cuts. After each cut was cleaned, the shepherd rubbed the lamb's woolly neck.

The little lamb snuggled down close to the sheep in the fold. With sleepy eyes the lamb looked to the shepherd as if to say, "It is good to be inside the fold."

The happy shepherd ran to tell his friends. "Come and give thanks with me," he shouted. "I've found my lost lamb."

The shepherd and his friends met to give thanks and praise. The little lamb was home at last.

Kangaroos and Koalas

Gail Fitzgerald

Jumpers

Homes come in many sizes and kinds. Homes can be big or small. Some homes are made of bricks. Others are made of logs. A home can be a place for many or just for one.

People live in homes, and many animals do too. Some baby animals have homes that move. Their homes give them everything they need for eating, sleeping, and keeping dry. Two animals in Australia have this kind of home.

A baby kangaroo's home is his mother's pouch. This baby is very small when he is born. He is smaller than the littlest finger on a child's

hand. After sixteen weeks he will open his eyes and peek out of his home. After twenty-five weeks he will leave his mother's pouch. His home will have become too small.

The kangaroo may grow to be seven feet tall, not quite as tall as a living room wall in a house. His tail will be more than three feet long, and it will be very strong. It would not be good to be in the way when he twitches that big tail!

The kangaroo's back legs are big and strong. With those strong legs he can hop very fast. He can even leap a wall that is nine feet tall or a puddle that is twenty-five feet wide. The kangaroo needs this speed and ability to help him get away from an enemy. But if he is cornered, he will use his strong back legs to protect himself. One kick can kill an animal or even a man!

The kangaroo also uses his legs for playing. One game he likes to play is tag. But boxing is the game he likes best.

Climbers

Here is one other baby that has a home that moves around. He may look like a stuffed animal, but he is not. This cuddly-looking animal is a koala.

Like the kangaroo, a koala is less than one inch long when he is born. He too will stay in his mother's pouch for twenty-five weeks. Then his mother will give him a ride on her back. Little by little he will become a strong climber. His sharp claws will help him hang on to the branches.

He will need those sharp claws for the rest of his life. The koala spends all his time in eucalyptus trees. He never eats anything but eucalyptus leaves. And he always eats those by biting off a leaf at the stem. He eats the leaf from the bottom to the top.

In Australia, *koala* means "no drink." The koala does not drink much water. He gets all the water he needs from the leaves of trees. That is why the koala hardly ever comes down from the trees.

The koala even sleeps in the trees. He can close his eyes and sleep on a branch. And he will not fall off while he is sleeping!

The kangaroo and the koala come from the same kind of home. But they live very different lives. Both are well known by the people in Australia.

Kate Kangaroo

Karen Wilt

illustrated by
Stephanie True

Work to Do

The sun shone brightly into the Kangaroos' grass hut.

"Kate," Kit called. "Time to get up."

Kit hopped to the kitchen. Mom was baking muffins. Dad was reading the paper.

When the muffins were baked, Dad called Kate again. She hopped slowly to her seat, yawning and stretching.

After they had all eaten, Dad said, "We have
work to do today. Who will help?"

"I will," said Kit.

"I will," said Kate.

Mom made box lunches for the three
workers. Off they hopped to a grassy plot of
land. The grass there was taller than Dad.

"Our roof is getting holes in it," Dad said.
"We must cut this grass to put on the roof.
When you have cut a bundle, bring it to me
right away."

They began snipping. Kate snipped fast.
She tied up a big bundle of grass.

"I'm tired and hot," she said to herself. "I'll take a swim in the pond; then I will take my bundle to Dad." Kate hopped to the pond, leaving her bundle behind.

At noon Dad stopped for lunch. "Where is Kate?" he asked.

"Here I am," Kate called, shaking off water at every hop. "I'll get my bundle of grass."

But when she looked, she could not find it anywhere. A grasshopper sat munching on a blade of grass where Kate had left the bundle. "Have you seen my bundle of grass?" Kate asked.

The grasshopper nodded. "Was that yours? It was not for lunch? My friends and I just finished eating it."

"Oh, no!" Kate hopped sadly back to Kit and Dad. She explained what had happened. "Next time I will finish my job," she said.

The Kangaroos ate their lunches. Then Dad picked up his grass bundles. "Now we have to fix the roof. Who will help me?"

"We will," said Kit and Kate. Kit picked up his bundle.

Kate Stops Again

Kate hopped happily down the path beside Dad and Kit. She would finish the job this time.

Dad climbed up the ladder to take off the torn roof. "I need some tar for the roof," he said. "Tar will keep out the rain."

"We will get it," Kate and Kit said. They each got a bucket and hopped to the tar pit. Quickly they filled the buckets with tar and began to drag them home.

But soon Kate hopped slower and slower. The tar was sticky and smelly. It was hard to carry the bucket down the road.

"Come on, Kate!" said Kit.

"You take your bucket to Dad. I will rest for a while," said Kate.

"Do not take too long," called Kit as he hopped away.

Kate stopped by a shady tree. "It is cool here," she said. She put her bucket down and stretched out on the grass. Soon she was sound asleep.

When Kit got back to the house, Dad put the tar on the roof. Just as he was about to tar Kate's room, the last of the tar dripped out of the bucket.

Dad waited for Kate. Kate did not bring her bucket of tar back. "We will not be able to tar Kate's room if she does not come soon," said Dad.

Just then a raindrop hit his nose. And another fell in the empty bucket. Dad climbed down the ladder. He and Kit rushed inside as the rain fell harder and harder.

A Lesson for Kate

The rain woke Kate up. She hopped home, leaving the tar bucket behind.

Kate went into the kitchen. Today was Mother's cleaning day. Kate was supposed to help clean the kitchen. The dishes from that morning lay piled in the sink. Kate had left them there.

Kate had not shelled the peas Mother had picked. The water pitcher sat on the counter waiting to be filled. Kate hopped into the living room. Dad, Mom, and Kit were talking about the work they had finished. Kate hung her head. She hopped quietly to her room.

Kate sat down to think. Plop! A drop of
water fell on her foot. She looked down and
saw a puddle at her feet. Raindrops fell on her
bed and on her books.

Kate hopped into the living room. "Rain is
coming in my room," she said. "My roof does
not have tar on it."

"I'm sorry, Kate. I ran out of tar when you did not bring me your bucket," Dad said. "Stay in the living room and you will not get wet."

Kate sat and thought. Her nose quivered sadly. The rain came down harder and harder.

Dad and Mom went to sleep. Even Kit fell asleep. But something was bothering Kate. She could not rest.

She had not taken her bundle of grass to Dad. She had not brought the tar. She had not cleaned the kitchen. She had not finished her jobs. "I never finish what I begin," she said sadly.

Finish What You Start

Kate hopped outside. The rain had stopped. Kate hopped to get the tar bucket she had left by the tree. She climbed up the ladder. Quickly she dripped the tar on the roof of her room. She climbed back down and cleaned up the rain puddles in her room.

Everyone was still asleep.

Kate hopped to the kitchen. She cleaned out the sink and did the dishes. She shelled the peas and made a salad.

Kate set the table. She took the pitcher to the brook to get some fresh water.

Dad woke up. He heard Kate hop out of the kitchen. Kit and Mom heard her too. They hopped into the kitchen and looked around.

"Did Kate do this?" they asked each other.

Kate hopped in and set the pitcher of water on the table. "Hello," she said.

Mom smiled at Kate. "What did you do, Kate?"

Kate wiggled her tail so hard that it shook the table. "I've finished all the jobs I could think to do," she said.

Mom gave Kate a big hug. "I am proud of you, Kate!" she said.

"So am I," said Dad, smiling. "You have learned to finish the job."

Mice

Rose Fyleman
illustrated by Kathy Pflug

I think mice
Are rather nice.

Their tails are long.
Their faces small.
They haven't any
Chins at all.
Their ears are pink,
Their teeth are white,
They run about
The house at night.
They nibble things
They shouldn't touch,
And no one seems
To like them much.

But I think mice
Are nice.

131

Cheerful Chickadees

Karen Wilt / illustrated by Ruth Ann Ventrello

The Chickadee Feeder

"Let's go for a walk in the woods," said Dad. "Get your coats and boots." Mother gave Mark and Becky their mittens and waved good-bye.

A Saturday walk in the woods with Dad was always fun. He showed them many things— foxes' dens, birds' nests, and rabbits' holes. They even saw raccoon tracks beside a frozen puddle of water.

132

"Look at that pine tree," Dad said. "Maybe you will see some good friends of mine." They all stopped talking and stood still.

Before long, one little bird began to twitter, "Chick-a-dee-dee-dee." Soon many birds twittered around the tree. They pecked at the seeds in the pine cones.

"Chickadees," Becky said. "All in their tiny black hoods."

"That is part of their name. They are called black-capped chickadees," Dad said.

"Look!" Mark whispered. "One of them is hanging upside down."

134

"They do that, but they never fall," Becky said.

"It is hunting for insects in the bark," Dad said.

After a while they walked on. Becky and Mark looked for more chickadees. They counted sixteen of them, but they heard many more calling "chick-a-dee-dee-dee" from the treetops.

At last they turned to go home.

They walked by the pine tree where the chickadees were feeding.

"Look how fat they have become!" Mark said.

Dad chuckled. "They have put on winter coats! They ruffle and puff out their feathers till they are snug as can be. The feathers trap warm air next to their skin and keep winter air out."

"Could we feed them?" Becky asked.

"I could make a bird feeder from a box," Mark said.

"Yes, I think that would be fine," Dad said.

At home Mark went right to work. He cut out two holes in the sides of a milk carton. Dad put a wire hook in the feeder. Mark hung it in a tree. Becky put in the seed.

From the kitchen window Becky and Mark could peek at the feeder.

Chickadee Tamers

Many chickadees came to Becky and Mark's bird feeder. The birds twittered while Becky and Mark ate their oatmeal in the morning. The birds chirped while the children ate their sandwiches at lunch. But the chickadees ate the seed between meals too. Becky had to put out seed every day.

Sometimes Becky and Mark would sit in the yard when the chickadees came to the feeder. One day a chickadee sat on a branch of a cedar tree and looked at them. Mark whistled at it, and it seemed to whistle back.

Dad came outside and sat down beside Becky and Mark. The chickadees fluttered back and forth in the yard.

"Those chickadees have become tame," Dad said. "Do they land on your hand and take seed yet?"

"They would eat out of our hands?" Mark asked.

"They might," Dad said.

Becky and Mark grabbed some seed and stood next to the feeder.

They waited and waited.

Then they heard a "chick-a-dee-dee-dee."

A chickadee fluttered in a circle around Mark. It landed on his hand, took a seed, then fluttered away. Soon another one came and took one of Becky's seeds. It went to a tree and sang, "Chick-a-dee-dee-dee."

In a bit, Mother called them in for hot apple cider. They all sat by the window to see the birds. "It is snowing," Mother said.

"What will happen to the chickadees?" Becky asked.

"God takes care of all the animals, Becky," Dad said.

Mark smiled. "Dad, you said the chickadees ruffle their feathers and trap warm air next to their skin. Is that how God takes care of them?"

"Yes," Dad said, "God has given chickadees a way to protect themselves."

The snow fell all afternoon, but the chickadees twittered and played happily.

The snow kept falling all night.

The next morning Becky and Mark woke up to a bright white day. The sun had come out. The snowstorm had stopped.

Becky and Mark dressed and ate. Then they went outside to clean up the snow. The sun shone on the snow and made it sparkle like gems.

"If I were a giant, I would sneeze. Then all the snow would blow away!" Mark said.

Becky giggled. "But you are not a giant, Mark. You will have to clean up the snow anyway."

141

Mark brushed off the car. Becky cleaned the walk. "I'll clean the bird feeder," Mark said. He dusted off the snow. "Where are the chickadees today?" he asked. "I hope they did not freeze."

Just then they heard a "chick-a-dee-dee-dee." In the cedar tree sat a little black-capped bird waiting for some seed.

Becky ran inside to get some seed. When she came back, she held them out to the chickadee.

It landed gently on her fingers and picked out a big seed. Then it fluttered back to the cedar tree.

"Chick-a-dee-dee-dee," it sang.

"Those chickadees are happy all the time," Becky said. "They never seem to grumble." She put some seed in the feeder. "When I see them singing in the snow, I feel like singing too."

Mark said, "Me too. I think I'll try to be as cheerful as a chickadee."

Make Your Own Bird Feeder

illustrated by Kathy Pflug

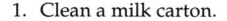

1. Clean a milk carton.

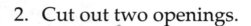

2. Cut out two openings.

3. Paint the outside of the carton.

4. Ask Mother or Dad to put a wire hook in the top.

5. Put birdseed inside the feeder and hang it outside near a window.

Owl Face

Eileen M. Berry

illustrated by
John Roberts

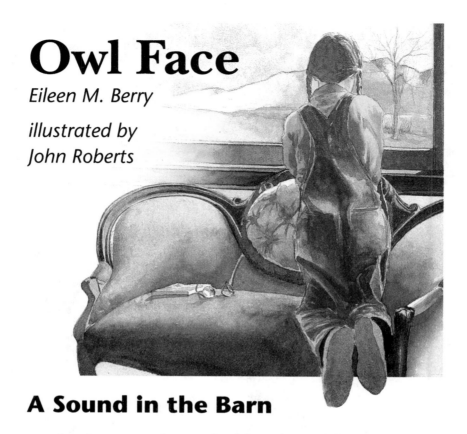

A Sound in the Barn

Amber put down her book and took off her new glasses. She gazed out the window, thinking that the sky looked like a puffy gray blanket.

With a blast of cold, Mom came in from outside. "Brrrr! It is freezing out there, Amber. Better put Buttercup in the barn. We might get snow tonight."

"Snow!" Amber jumped up. She grabbed her coat and scarf and put on her mittens. "May I take an apple to Buttercup?"

Mom smiled. "Catch." She tossed a red apple to Amber. "Where are your glasses, dear?"

Amber made a face. "They pinch my nose, Mom."

"We'll get them fixed," said Mom. "But for now, you need to keep them on."

Amber dashed over the grass to the barn. At least her glasses kept the wind from blowing in her eyes. She swung open the barnyard gate.

Her pony stood by the fence, close to the barn.

"Look here, Buttercup. See what I have for you?" She held up the apple.

Buttercup snorted. Amber patted her neck. "Come on inside, and you can eat it," she said.

Amber led Buttercup into the stall. She took a big whiff of the sweet hay. "Smells good," she said. "You will be warm and cozy tonight."

Amber brushed the pony's thick mane. "Know what, Buttercup? I hate these new glasses. They make me look funny."

Buttercup crunched the apple.

"Kim called me Owl Face today. And then the other girls said it too." She hung the brush up. "I wish I could smash my glasses."

Buttercup rubbed Amber's neck with her nose, sniffing. Amber giggled. "That tickles," she said.

Amber gave Buttercup a hug and turned to go. But a sound stopped her. It was like a little cry. The sound came again.

"What is that?"

Amber saw a small brown shape in the hay at the back of the stall. She bent down. It was a tiny barn owl.

Daddy Fixes Things

Amber knelt in the straw. "What's the matter, Little One? You must be hurt. Will you let me help you?"

The owl blinked. Its black eyes were bright in its white face. It tried to flap its wings. Only one wing flapped.

"Your wing is hurt," Amber said. She pulled off her scarf. "Come back to the house with me. Mom and Daddy will know what to do with you."

With gentle hands Amber folded the scarf around the owl. "There. It's like a little nest. You will have a warm ride."

Amber called to Buttercup. "Good night."

The first snowflakes were falling as Amber left the barn. She held the little owl close. She could feel it quivering. "It's all right," she said in a whisper. "I will take care of you."

Mom frowned when she saw the owl. "Where did you find it?"

"In the barn," said Amber. "Please let me bring him inside. It's so cold."

Mom dragged a box to the stove. "Put him in here. He will be close to the heat. We will see what your dad has to say." She placed a bit of screen over the top of the box.

Daddy looked at the owl for a long time. He felt the wing that would not flap.

"Will he die?" Amber asked.

"No," Daddy said. "Some tiny bones are broken. The owl will need a splint." He stood up. "Would you like to help me, Amber?"

"Yes!"

Amber helped Daddy rip up cloth into long strips.

"I will do the next part," Daddy said. Amber watched.

Daddy wore thick gloves to keep his hands safe from the owl's sharp beak. He bound the hurt wing to the owl's body with the strips of cloth.

"In a week or so, he should be fine," Daddy said.

Amber clapped her hands. "Can I keep him for a pet?"

Daddy's voice was quiet. "Owls don't make good pets, Amber. They are some of God's wild things. This owl would not be happy here. We will take him back to the barn soon."

Amber nodded. She gazed at the owl. "Daddy, do I have an owl face?"

Daddy smiled. "God gave you a girl face. He gave the owl an owl face. But both are very nice." Then he hugged her.

A New Name

Amber put on her glasses as soon as she woke up. Then she went to check on the owl.

"How do you feel, Little One?"

The owl was still.

"Oh. You are sleeping."

Mom grinned at Amber. "Owls like to sleep all day," she said. "Did you hear our friend hooting last night?"

"No." Amber giggled. "I hope that means he is better." She watched the owl. "I wish I could show him to my friends."

"Why don't you ask Kim to come over today?" said Mom. "She lives just up the road."

Amber did not look at Mom. She kept looking at the owl.

"You two could play in the snow," said Mom.

"Snow!" Amber ran to the window. The yard was a sea of white.

Amber turned back to Mom. "I would like to play in the snow," she said. "But Kim called me Owl Face."

Mom was very quiet for a long time. Then she said, "What do you think Jesus would do?"

Amber looked out at the snow. "I'll call Kim," she said.

The owl woke up soon. When Kim came, he was hopping around in the box. "You must have made him better," said Kim. "He looks like he feels fine."

"Daddy said he will need the splint for a few days. Then we will take it off and put him back in the barn."

"Let's give him a name," said Kim. "Do you like the name Smarty?"

"Yes," said Amber.

"Owls are smart," said Kim. "You look smart too, Amber, in your glasses. That's why I called you Owl Face. But you don't look like an owl."

Amber glanced at Mom. Mom smiled.

"Smarty," said Kim, "you have a very nice face."

Smarty flapped one wing. The two friends giggled. Smarty hooted, loud and long.

Be Wise About Owls

Eileen M. Berry

What Owls Look Like

Some owls are brown and white. Some are gray. One kind of owl, the snowy owl, is pure white with dark flecks. The barn owl has a white face shaped like a heart.

Snowy owl (top), barn owl (bottom)

Owls can be big or small. The great horned owl grows to be twenty-five inches tall. The elf owl does not grow over six inches tall.

Great horned owl chicks

A Boreal owl, a screech owl, and a great horned owl

Most owls have wide, yellow eyes. We say that their eyes make them look wise. But their eyes also help them to see very well at night.

Owls cannot look from side to side without turning their heads. But God made them able to turn their heads nearly all the way around so that they can see what is behind them.

Great horned owl

Owls hear through slits on the sides of their heads. The great horned owl and the screech owl have long tufts of feathers that look like ears, but they do not hear with them.

Barn owl

What Owls Do

Owls make many sounds. Some owls make a sound like a girl screaming. Some owls make a long, low sound like a person asking, "Whooooo?"

Owls hunt for their food at night. They like to eat mice, rats, snakes, rabbits, and insects. Owls have sharp beaks and claws to help them kill and eat their food.

Long-eared owl

161

Owls make their nests in trees, rocks, and barns. The snowy owl lives in the far north where the snow is. The elf owl lives in very hot, dry places.

Not every bird is a friend to the owl. Crows, jays, and hawks do not like owls. When one of these other birds is close by, owls sit very still. Some owls can close their eyes and blend in with the tree or rock where they are sitting. God has made the owl able to hide in plain sight.

An elf owl inside a cactus (top) and a spotted owl (bottom)

Digger Does It

Wendy M. Harris / illustrated by Johanna Berg

Waiting

"Digger, take it." Digger took one end of a rope in his mouth. The other end was tied to a basket. Digger held his end of the rope fast and pulled.

Digger pulled the basket to Brad. He wagged his tail.

"Good Digger. Drop it."

Digger let go and wagged his tail harder. Brad took his baseball cap out of the basket and put it on. "Let's see if anyone has started a game." He looked out the window. Two boys across the street in the park were tossing a ball back and forth.

The telephone rang. "Brad, would you get that?" his mother called.

"Yes, ma'am," he replied. "Digger, phone." Digger trotted into the hallway. He came back with the cordless phone and brought it to Brad.

"Good boy, Digger. Drop it." Digger dropped it in Brad's hand. Digger went to the window and sniffed. He sneezed and sat down.

"Hello. Dad! How is your trip so far? When are you coming home?

Two more weeks! Oh, the new house is nice. Yes, I'm helping. Digger does too." Digger looked at Brad. Brad's mother came into the room. "I miss you too. Yes, I will. Here's Mom." He handed the phone to his mother.

Brad looked out the window again. "Two more weeks. It can't wait that long," he whispered. "Digger, leash." Digger stood up, shook himself, and trotted out of the room.

"Mom, I want to take Digger on a walk. Just to the park." His mom winked and nodded. Digger came back holding the leash and wagging his tail.

Meetings

Digger walked beside Brad's wheelchair into the park. When they were in the right place Brad said, "Digger, stop." Digger sat down. Brad's baseball glove was in his lap. He used to play tee ball and hit from a tee. He was too old for that. He wanted to hit balls from a pitcher. Brad and Digger watched the two boys playing ball.

The two were no longer tossing the ball back and forth. One was pitching while the other one swung a bat. When the ball was hit, the boy pitching would chase after it. Digger saw the ball sailing, then rolling on the ground. He liked chasing balls when Brad played tee ball at home. Digger whined and wanted to go for the ball. His tail was wagging. Brad waited and watched.

Then one ball was hit very hard. The pitcher groaned as he watched it roll far from him. The ball was far from the pitcher but close to Brad. This was what Brad had waited for. He pointed to the ball. "Digger, take it." Digger bounded to the ball in the grass. He picked it up and trotted back to Brad. He dropped the ball in Brad's hand. Brad threw it back to the boys.

"Thanks," called the pitcher. The two boys walked over to meet Brad. "My name's Troy. He's Mike." It wasn't long until the three boys were all playing ball. Troy and Mike took turns pitching and batting. Brad fielded the balls with Digger's help.

"Brad," called Mike, "can you bat?" Brad smiled.

Surprises

"Dad! I'm glad you're home!" Brad hugged his father. Digger pranced around in circles.

"It's good to be home again! Even if it is a new home for us," said Dad. "I've missed you!" he added. Digger barked. "And you too, Digger! I've missed you too. Good dog!" Dad let go of Brad and patted Digger.

Dad got home just before dinner. They all sat down to eat, and Digger lay down on his rug.

"I don't have to leave anymore this summer! Now Brad can learn to bat," said Dad. "I didn't forget. We'll start tonight. And I have surprises for everyone, even Digger!" Digger looked at Dad. He barked, and everyone laughed.

After dinner, they cleared the table. Mom put the food away. Dad took dishes to the sink. Brad loaded them into the dishwasher. Soon the job was done, and Dad got out the surprises. Brad's surprise was a new baseball bat.

"I know we're getting a late start in teaching you to bat, Brad. But there is still time before the summer games start. We can play every evening."

"Thanks for the bat. I have a surprise for you too," said Brad. "But I'm saving it for later."

Outside, Dad showed Brad how to hold the bat. "Keep your eye on the ball. This isn't like tee ball." Dad backed up and pitched. Brad hit the ball high over Dad. He looked at Brad with wide eyes.

Brad laughed and shouted, "That's your surprise!" Digger trotted after the ball. His tail was wagging.

Service Dogs

Wendy M. Harris

Only a special kind of dog will make a good service dog. That is what a dog that helps people is called. A service dog must like to work and must be large enough to pull a wheelchair. It must be healthy and friendly. It must be smart and watch what people do.

Trainers use any breed of dog that can work well. Even mixed breeds can be service dogs. Do you think your dog would make a good service dog?

Service dogs go to school for a long time. They are trained to help people with disabilities. Trainers teach the dogs to pick up books, pencils, and even paper. Some service dogs pull wheelchairs. Some can open doors. Some dogs can even turn lights on and off.

A service dog has a leash. It also has a harness. Some dogs have backpacks to hold things for their owners. Some dogs use a strap to open doors. Some hold soft ropes to help their owners get out of wheelchairs.

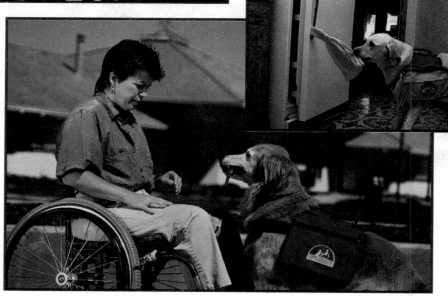

If you see a big service dog, don't be frightened. They have good manners and will not hurt you. They are gentle and will not bite. Show that you have good manners too. Don't pet a service dog without asking first. The dog is working and should not play. If the owner lets you pet the dog, pet him gently. Tell him what a good dog he is.

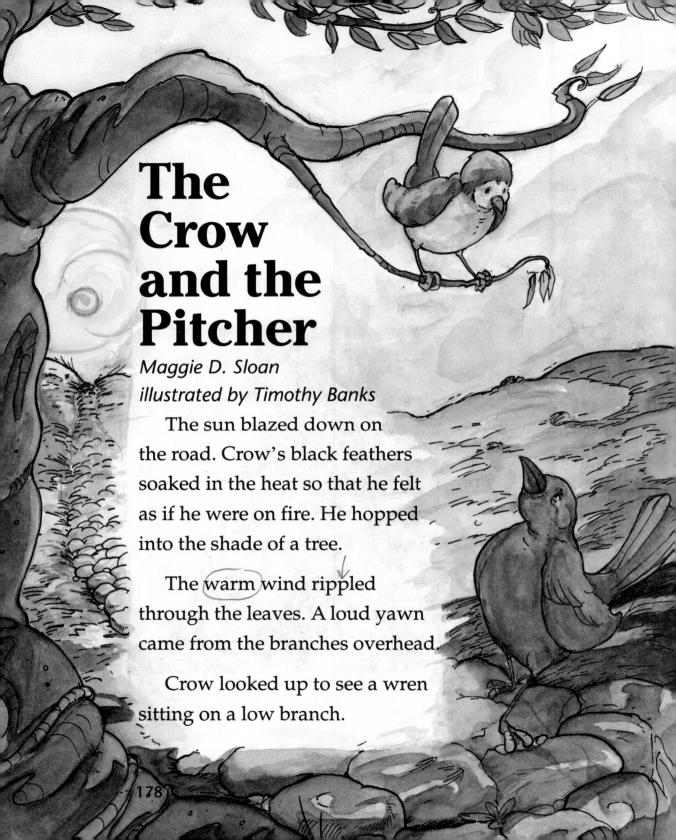

The Crow and the Pitcher

Maggie D. Sloan
illustrated by Timothy Banks

The sun blazed down on the road. Crow's black feathers soaked in the heat so that he felt as if he were on fire. He hopped into the shade of a tree.

The warm wind rippled through the leaves. A loud yawn came from the branches overhead.

Crow looked up to see a wren sitting on a low branch.

"Scorching indeed!" said Wren. "Makes it mighty hard to take a nap." He fluttered down to the ground and blinked at Crow. "You new to these parts?"

Crow nodded. "Yes, sir. I'm headed to Buttercup Bluff." He watched a cloud of dust swirl to the sky and scatter. "Is it always so hot here?" he asked. "I'm very thirsty! Where can I get a drink of water?"

Wren pecked at an ant but missed. "Well," he said, "there is a pitcher near what used to be the brook. It has water inside, but I don't think you can get to it. I have tried. Come, and I will show you."

The crow flapped his wings and ruffled his dusty feathers. He hopped slowly to the pitcher. Deep inside lay some water.

"Water!" he said. He tried to bend down, but he did not want to get his head stuck.

"You see?" said Wren, tapping his foot. "You can't reach down. You can't tip it, for the water will spill on the ground and be lost." Wren marched around the pitcher.

Crow looked about. "Aha!" he said, spying some pebbles. He flew and picked one up. Plunk! He dropped it into the pitcher.

"What are you doing?" said Wren, watching Crow get more pebbles and then drop them into the pitcher. Plunk! Plunk! Bit by bit the water rose to the top.

He stopped and perched on the rim once more. He took a drink of the cool water now at the top of the pitcher. "Come and drink, Wren," he said. "See? Little by little does the trick."

Wolf Pack
(a true story)

Karen Wooster

illustrated by Del Thompson
and Roger Bruckner

Happy Birthday

Welcome to Lapland. It is winter here now.
The woods and hills are still under the snow.
The streams and lakes are filled with ice. The
sky doesn't stay light for long. When it is dark,
the wolves come out for food. I am glad I am
safe at home by then!

Yesterday was my birthday. I haven't ever
had a birthday as exciting as the one yesterday.
I think I was the happiest girl in Lapland.

When morning rays of sunshine lit up the sky, Mother and Father tiptoed into the kitchen. I was sleeping on a wooden bed in the corner.

My sleepy eyes opened when I heard them singing. Mother and Father were standing at my bedside. Their eyes sparkled as they sang a song to wake me.

In her hands Mother held my birthday tray. She put it on my bed. Cookies, coffee, and lighted candles were on the tray. Father was carrying the gifts.

Waiting to open the gifts was hard. When my treat was finished, I picked up the first present. It was soft. The paper crackled and crunched as I tore it off. Inside was a bright red stocking cap. Mother had knitted it for me. It was a perfect fit. The big tassel on top bounced as I walked.

Next I opened the big gift. Father had made a sled for me. The sled was painted red to match my cap. What fun it would be to go sledding down the hill!

"Thank you, Mother and Father. This is really a happy birthday," I said as I smiled.

Mother said my smile was so big she could not see my face. Somehow, I know my smile did not hide my eyes.

Before Father left for his job, we sat down for Bible reading. Then we prayed as we did every morning. With his deep voice Father began reading a verse. "He shall call upon me, and I will answer him. I will be with him in trouble." For some reason, that verse stuck in my mind.

Sledding

It wasn't long before I was dressed and out in the snow. The tassel on my red cap bounced as I dashed off with my sled. I played on the frozen lake beside the house. I had to be careful not to fall into the holes. Father had cut them last night to get water for the animals.

After lunch I decided to try riding my sled down the hill. Up, up I went, dragging the sled behind me. The top was not far away now. The white valley and the lake spread before me. Then I heard a howl. Anyone in Lapland knows the howl of hungry wolves. Chills ran up and down my back as the dreaded cry came again.

A wolf doesn't often come out in the daytime. This howl could mean just one thing. These wolves were looking for dinner.

Wolves

As I turned, I saw the wolves by the edge of the woods. I saw one and then another and another. There were at least six wolves. Their eyes flashed as they began to run toward me. The biggest wolf led the pack.

I flung myself on my sled. As I sped down the icy hillside, I remembered the Bible verse Father had read after breakfast. "He shall call upon me, and I will answer him. I will be with him in trouble."

"Dear Lord," I prayed, "please help me not to be afraid. Keep me safe. Amen."

The verse said God would take care of me. I just didn't know how He would do it. Ahead of me lay the shiny lake and the safety of home. Behind me I could hear the heavy breathing of the wolves.

I thought I could reach the lake beside the house. The sled would slide easily on the ice. But I didn't know what might happen next.

Crash! Splash, splash, splash! What a loud noise!

Mother came running. I had fallen off my sled. Ouch! What a bump on my head!

Mother knelt and put her arms around me. "God is so good to us!" she said. "The wolves fell into the holes Father cut for water last night."

"You are right, Mother," I agreed. "God was very good to me on my birthday. You gave me a red cap. Father gave me a fast sled. And God gave the verse I needed even before I needed it. This will be a birthday I will never forget!"

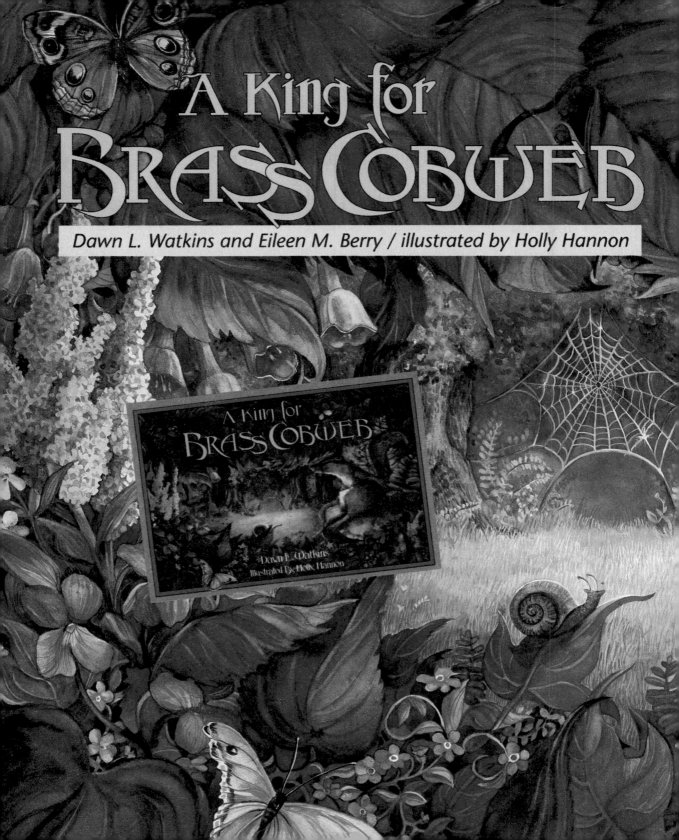

A King for BRASS COBWEB

Dawn L. Watkins and Eileen M. Berry / illustrated by Holly Hannon

Cast

Crab	Chipmunk	Lizard	Band of Raccoons
Rat	Grandmother	Fox	Turtle
Ant	Cricket	Rabbit	Snake
Bass	Hoot (an owl)	Big Raccoon	Narrator

Act I

(Crab, Rat, Ant, Bass, Chipmunk, and Grandmother Cricket are seated in the center of the stage.)

Narrator: The Kingdom of Brass Cobweb had many wonderful things. It had purple grass in the Dale of Snails. It had a pink mist over Mint Lake every morning. The clear water of Mint Lake tasted like cold peppermint tea. The kingdom also had a wonderful gate. It was a giant, shining cobweb of brass. But the Kingdom of Brass Cobweb had no king. One day, some of the kingdom's citizens were talking at Glass Pond.

Crab: We must have a king.

Rat: A king?

Ant: A king?

Bass: A king?

Crab *(firmly)*:
A king! This can't be the Kingdom of Brass Cobweb without a king!

Grandmother Cricket *(clicking tongue)*: A king might tax us.

Rat: That's right. The taxes might be high. Then we'd have to sell the great brass gate to pay the taxes.

Chipmunk *(quietly)*: Then we'd have a king, but we wouldn't have a kingdom. *(sighs)*

Bass: Let's search for a king. We'll let him run Glass Pond and Duck Dock. We'll see then how the taxes will be.

Rat: Yes.

Crab: Yes.

Ant: Yes.

Bass: Yes.

Ant: We've never had a king. How will we know who to look for?

Crab: Grandmother Cricket can tell us. She knows many things.

Narrator:

Grandmother
Cricket was the wisest in Brass Cobweb.
She had read many books and had traveled
to many places. She understood how things
change and how things stay the same.

Grandmother Cricket (*clicking tongue*)**:**

The king must be brave. He must be wise.
He must be true.

Rat: We will have to go far to find such a king.

Ant: Grandmother Cricket can't make such a trip.

Crab: I have to stay by the water.

Bass: I must stay *in* the water.

Grandmother Cricket *(standing up)*: I think we should send Chipmunk.

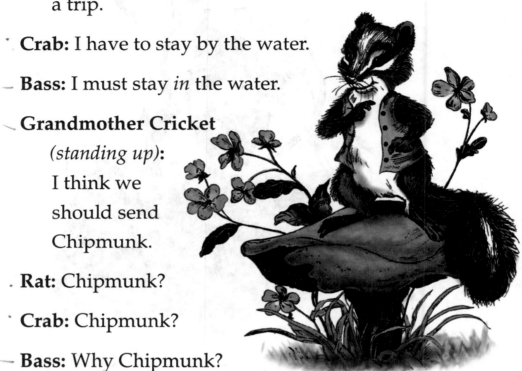

Rat: Chipmunk?

Crab: Chipmunk?

Bass: Why Chipmunk?

Grandmother Cricket: Chipmunk isn't old like me. He isn't small like Ant. He doesn't need to stay by the water. And he doesn't think of himself. He should go for us. *(taps cane)*

Bass, Crab, Ant, and Rat *(together)*: Yes! Send Chipmunk!

198

Chipmunk *(standing)*: I will go. I'll try to find us a good king.

Grandmother Cricket: Go as far as Seven Copper Hills. Or go as far as a month will take you. Then come back, with or without a king.

(Grandmother Cricket, Rat, Crab, Ant, and Bass wave to Chipmunk.)

Chipmunk *(waving)*: Farewell.

Act II

(Chipmunk strolls slowly across stage.)

Narrator: Chipmunk walked along Hemlock Highway. He saw meadows full of woolly sheep. He saw mines with violet stones and chunks of gold. He saw a glen deep with blue snow. On the fifth day he came to some thick woods. The yellow trees swayed in an easy breeze.

Hoot (*hidden among trees*):

> Hoot. Hoot.

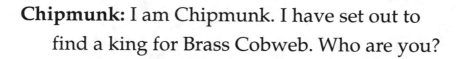

Chipmunk:

> Who is there?

Hoot: Hoot.

Chipmunk: I am Chipmunk. I have set out to find a king for Brass Cobweb. Who are you?

Hoot (*coming out from behind the trees*): Hoot. I am Hoot. That is my name. Where is Brass Cobweb?

Chipmunk: Five days down the road.

Hoot: Will you go far?

Chipmunk: As far as I must.

Hoot: I will come with you.

Narrator: Hoot and Chipmunk traveled all day. At night Hoot found a tree with thick branches for himself and a snug hole for Chipmunk. They fell asleep.

*(Hoot and Chipmunk sit
on two high stools among the trees. Lizard, offstage, cracks
a stick against the stage.)*

Hoot *(whispering)*: What is it?

*(Lizard comes out from behind the trees and keeps on hitting
the trees with the stick.)*

Hoot: Hoot.

Lizard *(looking up)*: Aha! There *are* beggars in
    my woods. I am king here. You're on my
    land. I am going to put you in jail.

Hoot: Tell me just what your law says.

Lizard: It says that no one may be on my land.

Hoot: Then you can't put us in jail.

Lizard *(yelling)***:** What? Why not?

Hoot: We are not on your land. We're in a tree.

(Lizard begins to climb toward them.)

Hoot: Get on my back, Chipmunk. We must be going.

(Hoot, carrying Chipmunk piggyback, runs away.)

Chipmunk: You are true and wise, Hoot.

(Sound effect: From offstage, a loud crack of thunder.)

Hoot: What was that?

Chipmunk: Just thunder. Thunder far ahead.

Hoot: A storm is coming! I am afraid of rain. I must go home!

(As thunder cracks again, Hoot turns, letting Chipmunk slide off his back.)

Chipmunk: Help! Help!

Narrator: But Hoot heard only the thunder. His fear got the best of him. He flew toward his yellow woods.

(Hoot runs back behind the trees.)

Act III

(Chipmunk sits down and leans back against Fox.)

Narrator: Chipmunk landed on something warm and soft.

Fox: Oh, my! Who are you?

Chipmunk: I am Chipmunk from Brass Cobweb. I fell off an owl.

(Chipmunk and Fox stand and face each other.)

Fox: What are you doing here?

Chipmunk: I'm on a trip.

Fox: I like to take trips. I'll go with you.

(Fox and Chipmunk start walking.)

Narrator: Soon Fox and Chipmunk found some stones in a cave. The stones had sharp prickles all over them. They asked a rabbit what the stones were.

Rabbit (*holding out stones*): They're seeds. They grow into hills overnight. You may take some.

(*Fox puts the seeds into his sack. They walk on.*)

Fox (*pointing*): Look! Corn! Let's have breakfast!

Chipmunk: We must pay. It's not ours.

Fox (*grabbing an ear of corn*): We'll pay.

(Big Raccoon and his Band drop a net over Fox and Chipmunk from behind.)

Big Raccoon: Here are the robbers. Tie them up!

(Raccoons tie Fox and Chipmunk to a tree. Big Raccoon holds up Fox's sack.)

Big Raccoon:
What's in here? My corn?

Fox: No, just nuts and seeds. Don't do anything to those seeds.

Big Raccoon: Seeds for what?

Fox: Never mind. Just don't plant them.

(Big Raccoon talks to his Band in a huddle. They start planting the seeds.)

Chipmunk: You are clever, Fox. And brave to try a trick when you are tied up.

(Raccoons finish planting the seeds. Chipmunk, Fox, and Raccoons all go to sleep.)

(Stage lights off.)

Chipmunk: Fox! It's working! The hills are
   growing!

Fox: Here's our chance! The tree will fall over.
   We'll slip the rope off and run!

(Sound effect: Loud crash. Stage lights on again.)

*(Fox and Chipmunk
run across the stage.
Chipmunk trips and
falls.)*

Chipmunk: Help!
   Fox, wait for me!

(Fox runs offstage.)

Chipmunk
   *(yelling
   after him)***:**
   You are no
   true friend!

(*Raccoons, carrying swords, surround Chipmunk.*)

Big Raccoon: Chipmunk! You ruined our field with these hills.

Chipmunk: I didn't plant the seeds. You did.

Big Raccoon (*to other Raccoons*)**:** Which of you planted the seeds?

(Raccoons all shout and point at each other. They begin fighting each other with swords. Chipmunk wiggles through the fight and runs away.)

Act IV

(Chipmunk sits onstage. Turtle kneels close by with his head on the ground, face hidden.)

Narrator: Chipmunk sat by a small lake. He thought of Mint Lake and Glass Pond. He wanted to go home.

Chipmunk *(sadly)*: I can't go home. I haven't found a king.

Turtle *(sitting up)*: What's that you say?

Chipmunk *(startled)*: I'm Chipmunk from Brass Cobweb. I am looking for a king. Who are you?

Turtle: I am Turtle. How far will you go to look for a king?

Chipmunk: I'll go to Seven Copper Hills.

Turtle: Well, you're not far from there. I can take you to the hills. Would you like a ride across Wonder Lake?

(Chipmunk rides on Turtle's back across stage, then hops off.)

Chipmunk: Thank you for helping me. You are true and brave.

Turtle: Maybe so. But I think we are lost.

(Snake sneaks up from behind the two.)

Snake: Are you lossst?

Turtle: Yes! Can you help us?

Snake: Come thisss way. I'll ssshow you where to go.

*(Chipmunk and Turtle
turn away from Snake
and whisper.)*

Turtle: Let's go
with him!
Snake will
help us.

Chipmunk: No,
I don't trust
him.

Turtle: Come on!

Chipmunk: No.
It would not
be wise. Please take me back across the lake.

Chipmunk *(walking away from Snake)***:** Thanks
just the same, but I think we'll go this way.

*(Chipmunk climbs on Turtle's back and begins to ride back
across stage.)*

Snake (*calling after them*)**:** I'm sssorry you could not come with me. I was to have a feassst. Roassst turtle.

(*Snake exits, laughing.*)

Turtle: Thank you for helping me. You were right. I shouldn't have trusted Snake.

Chipmunk: Friends help friends. I must start for home now. Good-bye.

(*Turtle waves to Chipmunk. Chipmunk walks slowly away.*)

Act V

Narrator: Chipmunk was soon on his way. He was happy to be going home. But he was also a little sad. He had not yet found a king.

(Bass, Ant, Rat, Crab, and Grandmother Cricket take places at center stage again.)

Grandmother Cricket *(pointing)*: Look! Chipmunk has come home!

Chipmunk *(sadly, hanging head)*: I didn't find a king.

Rat: That's too bad. We've built him a fine house in Cricket Thicket.

Ant: Yes, and we've made him a wonderful crown.

Grandmother Cricket: Tell us of your trip.

Chipmunk: I found an owl named Hoot. He was wise and true but not brave. Then I found Fox. He was brave and wise but not true. Then I found Turtle. He was true and brave but not wise.

Narrator: Chipmunk spent a long time telling his friends all his adventures.

Rat: That was brave of you to fly with Hoot.

Crab: And you didn't trust Snake. That was wise of you.

Bass: And that was true of you to keep Turtle from harm.

Grandmother Cricket: You have brought us many good stories.

Chipmunk: But I did not bring a king.

Grandmother Cricket: Yes, you did. You brought us a king who is brave and wise and true.

Chipmunk: Who is it?

Bass, Ant, Rat, Crab, and Grandmother Cricket: You! You are the king for Brass Cobweb.

(Rat places the crown on Chipmunk's head. Ant, Bass, Rat, Grandmother Cricket, and Crab clap; then all join hands and circle Chipmunk as Narrator closes the play.)

Narrator: King Chipmunk went to live in the fine house in Cricket Thicket. He did not tax the kingdom. But he did brave deeds and gave wise answers and was always true to his friends. When anyone hears of Brass Cobweb now, he does not hear about the cobweb gate. He hears about the wise, true, brave king there. He hears of King Chipmunk.

Treasures

Jonathan's Treasure

Milly Howard and Susan W. Young

(based on historical research)

illustrated by John Roberts

Five Cents

Jonathan Goforth was born on his father's farm in Canada in 1859. He had nine brothers and one sister. Those were hard times for everyone in Canada. Many farm owners had no money to pay men to do farm work. It was a big help to Jonathan's family to have so many children. They all helped with the work on the farm.

When Jonathan was just a boy, a lady came
to visit.

"Would you like to see my chickens?"
Jonathan asked.

"That would be very nice,"
the visitor said. So after lunch
Jonathan took her through
the chicken house.

Soon the visitor was ready to leave. But just before the buggy rolled out of the yard, she gave him five pennies.

What a surprise! Jonathan had never had five cents of his own before.

"Mother!" he called. He ran up the steps, holding the five cents tightly. "The lady gave me five pennies! May I go to the candy store?"

"No, Jonathan," said his mother. "You cannot go today."

Jonathan looked up at his mother. "Please," he said.

"Jonathan, look." Mother gently turned Jonathan toward the road. The sky over the dark trees was pink. It was nearly time for the sun to go down.

"I see, Mother," he said. "It will soon be dark. I'll go first thing in the morning! I'll get up before daylight and do my chores!"

"Not in the morning, Jonathan. It's the Lord's Day," his mother said. "You will have to wait until next week to spend your five cents." Jonathan's mother gave him a hug and went inside the house.

The Candy Store

Jonathan sat down on the steps and leaned on the post. He didn't see the sky turn from pink to red. He didn't hear the wind in the trees.

All he could see in his mind was the candy store. He felt the five cents in his pocket.

In his mind he walked down the street to the candy store. He could hear the bell jingle as he walked inside. He could feel the pine boards under his bare feet. He could see the jars and jars of candy. There were lemon drops, orange suckers, and peppermint sticks. There was almost  everything a boy could wish for. For five cents he could get ten sticks of candy!

"Let me see," he thought to himself. "I'll start with peppermint, and then—"

Suddenly, Jonathan sat up straight. An offering was going to be taken the next day at church. It was to help send missionaries to far-off lands to preach the gospel.

"I should give my five pennies to the missionaries," he thought. "But the lady gave me the money to do what I wanted with it. And I want to buy some candy. Oh, why did I have to remember the offering now?"

Jonathan leaned on the post. He thought about the missionaries, and then he thought about the candy. He didn't know much about missionaries. But he knew all about candy. He started choosing his candy again.

"I'll start with peppermint and then—"
It was no use. He could not stop thinking about
the offering. "What could five cents do anyway
to tell someone about Christ?" he thought.
"It's too little."

The Battle

That night Jonathan put his five pennies on the table near his bed. Mother came to his room to tuck him in.

"Have you prayed yet, Jonathan?" Mother asked.

"No, Mother, I do not feel like praying tonight."

"What's wrong?" she asked. Jonathan shrugged.

"Are you angry?"

Jonathan shook his head.

"It's best to take care of whatever is bothering you before you sleep," his mother said. "Give it to God."

Jonathan hung his head. After Mother left, Jonathan tried three times to pray. But the most he could say was, "Dear Lord. . . ."

His heart was hurting.

Jonathan tossed and turned in his bed. He thought about the missionaries and the pennies. He thought about the candy and the people who needed to hear about Christ. He could not sleep. He thought and thought.

After a long time, he decided to give the pennies to the missionaries. At last he was able to pray. Jonathan smiled and fell asleep.

The sunshine woke Jonathan the next morning. He jumped out of bed and ran to the window. The milk pails rattled as his brothers did their chores in the barn. He dressed quickly and ran to join them. He had to work quickly to finish his chores.

He was the last one to slide into his place at the table.

"You're a little late today," his father said.

"Yes, sir. I slept late," Jonathan said.

The Offering Basket

When Jonathan was dressing for church, he saw the five pennies on the table. He picked them up to put them in his pocket. He wanted to give them to the missionaries, but he began to think about the candy again. He could almost taste the candy he wanted.

"Jonathan!" called his father.

Jonathan stuffed the pennies into his pocket as he ran outside. His brothers grabbed his arms and lifted him into the wagon. Then the wagon left, heading toward the church. Jonathan held on to keep from falling out. His family chattered happily, but Jonathan kept silent. He was thinking.

When they reached the church, Jonathan got out of the wagon last. He waited until the rest of his brothers walked in, and he went behind them.

While everybody else sang, Jonathan thought about the pennies. He thought and thought. Then he knew what he would do.

The time came to pass the offering basket.

Jonathan could hear clink after clink as people dropped in their offerings. When the basket reached his bench, he saw it pass from brother to brother. Everyone had something to give. The basket reached Jonathan. He opened his hand and dropped in the five pennies.

He passed the offering basket to his mother. She looked at him and smiled. Jonathan grinned. He was so happy he felt as if he had a whole store full of candy. His heart was not hurting anymore.

Jonathan Goforth:
Missionary to China

Susan W. Young
illustrated by John Roberts

Jonathan Goforth and his wife, Rosalind, went to China as missionaries in 1888. Mr. Goforth was 29 years old. For the next 47 years, Mr. Goforth would preach God's Word to tell the people of China about Christ.

The Goforths had been in China only a few weeks when a fire burned their house. Almost all the things they had brought from home were lost in the fire. Only Mr. Goforth's Bible and their money were saved. This was very hard for his wife, but Mr. Goforth told her that God would take care of them, even in China.

Mr. Goforth found it was not easy to speak Chinese. The sounds were not the same. The Chinese people could not understand him. Mr. Goforth asked God to help him. One day he told his wife that if God did not help him soon, he would not be able to preach anymore. That same day Mr. Goforth preached to some Chinese men. The men asked him to go on preaching. They were able to understand all that he said.

Two months later, Mr. Goforth got a letter. It told how some men had prayed for him one night. It was at the very time Mr. Goforth began to speak Chinese well. God had answered prayer.

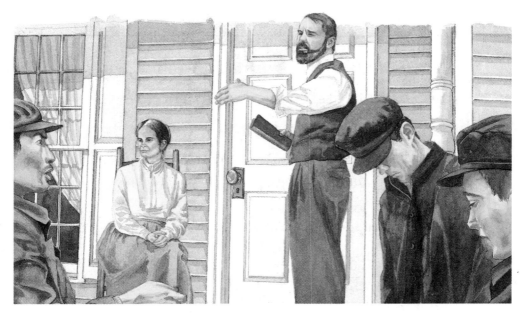

The Chinese people wanted to know all about the missionaries from another land. The Chinese people lived in paper houses and slept on mats. The missionaries lived in a wooden house and slept in beds. The people wanted to see the missionaries' house. Sometimes more than 500 people would stand outside the gate of the yard. Mr. Goforth would let them in a few at a time. He would tell them they could see the house if they listened to him preach. The people would listen and then go into the house to see how the missionaries lived. Many people heard about Christ this way.

When Mr. Goforth was not preaching, he would study his Bible. He had learned as a small child to read and learn verses. Before he died, he had read his Bible through 73 times. He had also read his Chinese New Testament through 60 times.

Three years before he died, Mr. Goforth lost the sight in his eyes. When he was 76, he went back to Canada to tell the people about his work in China. He had done what God had called him to do. He told others about Christ.

Captain Stripe's Gold

Milly Howard / illustrated by Tim Davis

The Trail

Zack Zebra trotted to the far end of the field. He tossed his head and looked back as the other zebras gathered around Captain Stripe.

He laughed at Captain Stripe's words. " 'Stay out of the jungle!' " he said to himself. "I get so tired of Captain Stripe's orders! Just because he is the new leader, he thinks that he knows everything."

Captain Stripe's father had once been the leader of the zebras and had taught his son well. No one had been surprised when Stripe became the leader.

"Captain Stripe does not have a son," Zack said to himself. "I will be the next leader of the zebras. Then I can do as I wish."

He looked at the trail leading into the jungle. "I'm thirsty," he said to himself. He looked back at the muddy stream where the zebras were drinking.

"That water is too muddy to drink," he said and trotted through the jungle. Branches hung over the trail, shutting out the bright sunlight.

Crack! Snap! Zack jumped as a huge head appeared between some branches. He looked at two big eyes and a long trunk.

"Where are you going?" asked Mumba, the elephant.

"I'm g-g-going to get something to drink," Zack said. He didn't want to say any more, so he trotted quickly away.

Mumba stood still until the trees hid Zack from sight.

As Zack trotted farther into the jungle, more and more vines and ferns crowded the trail. Zack had to slow down and walk around some of the vines. At last he heard water dripping.

"Water!" he said, walking toward the sound. He stopped at the edge of the river and bent to drink.

"Psst!" a voice said. Zack looked up. There was no one to be seen.

"You aren't very fffriendly, are you?" the voice said. Zack jumped back as a large vine dropped right down next to him. Two yellow eyes looked into his.

"How about thisss, Croc?" the vine said. "Here is a ssstriped horssse that cannot talk."

A log floated in the water near Zack's legs. It opened its eyes and looked at Zack sleepily.

"Cannot talk? What kind of beast is it?" it asked. The log yawned, showing yellow brown rows of sharp, pointed teeth.

Logs and vines that talk! Zack turned around quickly.

Gold!

"Do not run away," the voice said. "We will not hurt you. I'm Mona, the python," the voice went on. "Thisss is my friend Croc. We do not get many visssitorsss down here, do we, Croc?"

The crocodile sank a little lower in the water. "Not often enough anyway," he muttered with a hungry look in his eyes.

Croc looked at the zebra. "What are you doing in this part of the jungle?" he asked.

"I needed a drink," replied Zack, tossing his head. "I'm very thirsty."

"By all meansss drink until you are done," Mona said. She coiled up around another branch.

Zack stretched his neck carefully to drink from the river. "This river is nice," he said. "We just have brooks to drink from back in the fields. The water is often muddy from so many hooves walking in it. Why do you two have this river all to yourselves?" he asked.

"Well," Mona said. She paused and glanced slyly at Croc. "There are ssso many riversss here that everyone has hiss own watering place."

"Really?" asked Zack. "Why, this part of the jungle would be just the place for our herd. Captain Stripe is always looking for new watering places. Why doesn't he bring us here?"

The crocodile rolled his eyes at Mona. "Maybe he doesn't want you to know about the gold," he said.

"Gold?" asked Zack.

Mona swayed back and forth. "Oh, I thought everyone knew about the gold. Robberss hid it in a ssshady place many yearsss ago. Now the viness have hidden it from sssight. But I know where it isss." Her eyes glowed.

"All we need is a strong fellow like you to get it for us," said Croc. "We will gladly divide the gold with you."

Zack looked at the two comrades. There was something about them that bothered him. Zack almost seemed to hear Captain Stripe talking. He shook his head and put the voice out of his mind.

"Where is the gold?" he asked. "I'll help you get it. I'll take real gold to the zebras. They will not think Captain Stripe's words are so good then! I will not have to wait until I am older to be the leader!"

"You must crosss the bridge to the other ssside of the river," said Mona.

Zack looked at the old wooden bridge swaying across the river. "I do not think . . ." he began.

But Mona just laughed. "Are you really afraid?" she asked. "A leader cannot be afraid. It's a sshort trip. Sssoon you will be back with the gold."

The crocodile winked at Mona. "Bigger beasts than you have used the bridge."

Real Gold

Zack put one hoof on the bridge, then another one. The planks clattered under him as he moved. Creak! went the next board. He moved carefully on the bridge. But there were no boards for the next step. Zack looked down. He saw the hooded eyes of the crocodile looking up at him.

Zack stopped. Croc's eyes did not look friendly. Something about Croc and Mona still worried him.

"Come on! It's not far now." Croc blinked his yellow eyes. His tongue brushed across his mouth.

Zack did not move. Why did hardly anyone come to visit Mona and Croc? It was a peaceful place, and the water was good. Certainly the few visitors would have told others. Zack then had a horrible thought. What if none of the visitors were ever able to leave the area?

Zack backed off the sagging bridge. The empty bridge swayed back and forth. Suddenly it broke with a snap! Down it splashed into the water. The crocodile's mouth sprang shut on a plank.

"Ouch!" he cried, sinking into the water.

Zack turned around just as Mona dropped
over him. He kicked and kicked, but she coiled
around him tightly. There was no way to get
loose from her grasp.

"Oh, Captain Stripe," he thought to himself, "your words were better than real gold! How I wish I had listened to you!"

"Stop!" a voice said. It sounded like thunder as it rang through the jungle. Zack looked up at the huge elephant he had seen by the trail.

"Go away," Mona said.

"Let him go," Mumba said. "I could crush the likes of you under one of my feet."

He lifted one foot. Mona unwound slowly. She glared at the elephant and slithered away. "There will be another time," she said and was gone.

Mumba turned to Zack. "Is this where you came to drink? I thought Captain Stripe kept you all in the fields. There you would be safe from Mona and Croc."

"He does," replied Zack. He hung his head. "But I thought I was wiser than Captain Stripe. Now I know why he is the captain of the zebras and I'm not."

Mumba shook his head. "Captain Stripe thinks of your safety. He is a wise leader."

"I know now," Zack said. "I see why the other zebras listen to his words as if they were gold. They were better than real gold today."

"How much better is it to get wisdom than gold! and to get understanding rather to be chosen than silver!" Proverbs 16:16

The Fire Keeper

Milly Howard / illustrated by Tim Davis

The Fire

The smoke from the fire curled around Little Fox's head. He choked and fanned it away. "Just once I wish I could go on the hunt with the men," he said.

White Cloud, his mother, looked up from her bed of animal skins. She smiled at the small boy crouched over the fire.

"Then who would take care of me, Little Fox?" she asked. "Who would keep the fire going?"

Little Fox smiled back at her. He poked at the fire to make the orange flames burn more brightly. "I will, Mother. But soon you will be well. Then you will not need me to take care of you."

White Cloud moved her hurt leg under the skins. Little Fox looked up as she moaned.

"I should have gone with you to the spring. I would have killed that wild pig! Then he would not have hurt you."

He grabbed a spear from beside the wall and thrust it toward a shadow.

"There! He is dead!" Little Fox pretended. He leaned the spear against the wall.

White Cloud laughed at the boy. Little Fox was glad to hear her laughter for he knew how much she suffered. She could not stand on her leg. So Shining Star, his older sister, had gone to get water from the spring.

Little Fox sighed and picked up a small
stone. The men had gone on the hunt two days
ago. Little Fox wanted to go hunting, but all the
men thought he was too little. All he could do
was take care of the fire. He felt the end of the
stone. It was sharp enough. Little Fox began to
scratch on the wall of the cave with the sharp
stone. He moved the stone back and forth.

White Cloud saw the four legs of a buffalo appear. Then came its back. Soon its head looked down from the wall. How Little Fox could draw!

"Soon he will be old enough to go on the fall hunt with the men," she thought. "He will hunt the animals he draws so well." She closed her eyes and lay back on the bed.

Little Fox mixed the red clay with water. He picked up a brush. He had made it himself using fur and a stick. Carefully he painted the buffalo red.

The fire flickered as he dug out burnt sticks to mix with water and make black paint. "I'll add more branches to the fire soon," he said to himself, "but I'll finish my buffalo first."

He frowned at the stone bowl. There was not a drop of water left. "What is taking Shining Star so long?" he thought. "She should be back with the water."

He walked to the mouth of the cave. All he could see were the treetops far below. Little Fox turned back to his painting.

"There is no water to make paint," he
thought to himself. "I'll draw with the burned
tips of the sticks." He rubbed the sticks over the
buffalo. He worked slowly. He added a little
black here. He rubbed some out there. Then he
stepped back to look.

"There! It is done!" he said to himself. "Now
it looks more like a real buffalo."

Mountain Lion

"Little Fox!"

Little Fox dropped the burnt stick and ran to the mouth of the cave. Shining Star scrambled up the last few feet. She stumbled past her brother.

"Mountain lion!" Shining Star cried. She pointed down the side of the cliff. Little Fox could see the mountain lion leaping from rock to rock.

"What is it?" called her mother, trying to sit up. Shining Star ran to her side. "A mountain lion!" she cried.

"Use the fire to frighten him away!" White Cloud called to Little Fox.

Little Fox reached for one of the burning branches to frighten the mountain lion. But the fire had gone out!

The mountain lion leaped across the rocks. It landed in the mouth of the cave. There it crouched, snarling!

Little Fox felt for the spear leaning against the cave wall. His fingers closed around the spear. His mouth was dry. This was no game. The mountain lion was no shadow to kill!

Little Fox yelled as loudly as he could. He ran at the mountain lion and threw the spear. Surprised, the mountain lion stepped back. It lost its footing and slid down a few feet. The spear flew over its head. Then Little Fox heard shouts below. The hunters were home!

The mountain lion turned quickly. It leaped from the rocks and was gone. Little Fox stood still as his father climbed into the cave.

"I let the fire go out, Father." Little Fox hung his head. "I didn't think keeping a fire was as important as hunting."

His father stooped down. "You were wrong to let the fire go out, Little Fox. You are the fire keeper. What would we do without our fire? It warms us and protects us." He looked at the boy's bent head.

"But you were brave today, Little Fox. You will be a good hunter when you are a little older."

Little Fox lifted his head, and his eyes brightened. "You forgive me?" he whispered.

"Yes, but you must be the fire keeper until the hunt is over," his father replied.

"Oh, I will, Father!" Little Fox cried. "I'll keep the fire burning!" He ran to tend the fire. Soon Little Fox had the fire burning brightly.

That night Little Fox mixed his paints carefully. Before long a mountain lion glared down from the cave wall. Its yellow eyes glowed in the light of the fire. From then on, when Little Fox looked at the mountain lion, he remembered to tend the fire!

December Leaves

Kay Starbird
illustrated by Johanna Berg

The fallen leaves are cornflakes
That fill the lawn's wide dish,
And night and noon
The wind's a spoon
That stirs them with a swish.

The sky's a silver sifter
A-sifting white and slow,
That gently shakes
On crisp brown flakes
The sugar known as snow.

Gifts from the Wise Men

(taken from Matthew 2:1-12)

Becky Davis / illustrated by Del Thompson

A New Star

"Look! Look up in the sky! This is the brightest, most glorious star I have ever seen."

A wise man stood outside pointing to the sky and calling to his friends. Other wise men came hurrying out. Their eyes grew wide as they looked at the marvelous star.

"This is wonderful!" one friend said. "I have studied the sky for many years, but I have never seen anything like this. This star is

"It means that the King is born," another wise man said. The other men nodded when they heard these words. This was something they had read about and had waited for. "We must leave right away and go to the land where the star leads us," one said. "We will find the new King there."

"We do not know how long we will have to travel or how far we will have to go," said one of the men. "We will need many camels to carry our food and water. I will tell the servants what to pack."

As the servants packed the things needed for the trip, the wise men talked with each other.

"We will be seeing a very special King," said one. "We cannot go empty-handed."

"We must take Him our most precious gifts," agreed another. "But what will we take?"

All the wise men thought and thought, trying to decide what would be best to take to this special King.

"Everything is done," said the servants. "The camels are ready to go. We have packed plenty of food and warm blankets."

The wise men shook their heads. "But we do not have everything we need."

The servants were eager to help. "Is there anything else we can get for you?"

"No," came the reply. "There are some things that *we* must get. We must choose our best gifts to take to the new King."

The servants held the camels as the wise men walked slowly back inside.

"What treasures can we take?" the wise men wondered. "What can we take that would be good enough for this wonderful King?"

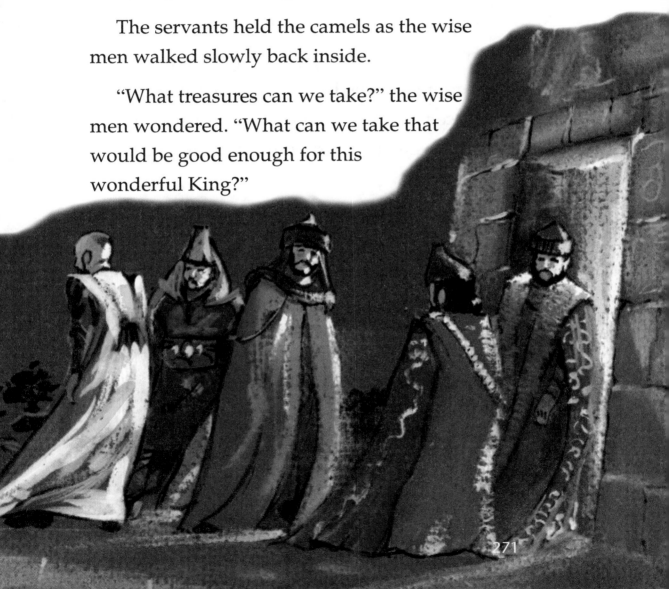

Treasures for the King

When the wise men came back outside, one was carrying something heavy. It was wrapped in a soft velvet cloth.

"Look!" he said to his friends. "I am going to take the new King a gift of gold."

"That is a generous gift," another agreed. "I am going to give the new King a gift of frankincense." He opened a little carved box. A fragrant smell drifted on the evening breeze.

"Your gifts are thoughtful ones," said another wise man. "I, too, have a gift." He held out a fine white bottle. As he opened the bottle, the sweet smell of myrrh filled the air.

"The King will be pleased with your gifts," said one of the servants. "But the trip will be a long and hazardous one. Robbers hide along the roadside to attack rich caravans such as yours. We will have to be alert at all times."

"Yes, you're right," said one wise man. "If they steal our food or other things, it will be bad, but at any cost we must keep them from stealing our gifts for the King."

The other men nodded. They knew that the gifts they were taking to the new King would be the most important things they carried.

Carefully the servants placed the precious gifts into the bags loaded on the camel's backs.

"Now we have everything we need," the wise men said. "We are ready to leave."

Once again the servants held the camels, and
the wise men climbed on. Then the wise men
and servants started toward Jerusalem.

Night after night the big brown camels plodded over the bleak desert. Sometimes the wise men rested or slept. But one of the servants would always stay awake to keep the treasures safe.

A Wicked Plan

When the small caravan reached Jerusalem, people stopped to look at it.

"What is that?" they whispered to each other.

"Important men who have come from a far land," others whispered back. "Why are they here?" But the children were not afraid. They ran alongside the camels to lead the wise men to the palace. There the wise men went in to see King Herod.

"Where is the new King of the Jews?" they asked Herod. "We have seen His star in the east and are come to worship Him. We know that He was born, but we cannot find Him. Can you tell us where He lives?"

King Herod did not reply right away. He began to walk back and forth. "If this new King is so well known, why have I not heard about Him?" he thought. "Will the people begin to follow Him instead of me?"

Then Herod turned to the wise men. "I will ask my chief priests and scribes where the new King was born."

Herod's scribes gathered to look in the temple scrolls. "We read here that the new King will be born in Bethlehem," they told Herod and the wise men.

The angry king left the room. "I should have heard about this new King!" he shouted. "Is He really more important than I am?" Herod's eyes grew dark. "I am afraid of this King. I do not want the people to worship Him when they should be worshiping me. I will not let them do it!"

Then the evil king thought up a wicked plan. He laughed and rubbed his hands together. Then he came back to the wise men and smiled at them. "Go to Bethlehem and find the child," he said. "Then come tell me where He is. I want to worship Him too."

The wise men did not know that Herod really planned to kill the new King. They bowed low before the king and went out. Leaving the palace, they headed toward Bethlehem, following the bright star.

The camels plodded through the quiet streets of Bethlehem. The tired men rode silently, following the moving star.

"Look!" called the first man when they had gone a little farther. "The star has stopped over that house."

Precious Treasure

The wise men knew they had reached the end of their trip. They rejoiced with new strength and energy. "We have found the place. Let us go in and worship the King!"

When they entered the house, they saw Mary and a young child.

"Is this child the new King?" they asked.

"Yes, he is," replied Mary. "And His name is Jesus."

The wise men bowed low before Jesus.

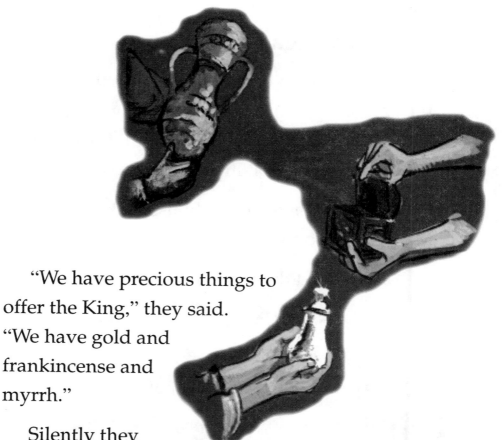

"We have precious things to offer the King," they said. "We have gold and frankincense and myrrh."

Silently they placed their gifts before the young child. Silently they worshiped Him.

As the wise men rose to leave, Mary and Joseph thanked them for the gifts.

The wise men bowed again. "We wanted to bring our most precious treasures to give to the King."

The wise men led their camels through the streets of Bethlehem. At the city gates, the men climbed onto their beasts. They turned the camels toward their own country.

"We must go back to Herod," one wise man said suddenly. "Remember, he wants to worship the new King too."

So the caravan turned around to travel back to Jerusalem. But that night all the men had a dream. The next morning one said, "I dreamed something last night that troubles me. I dreamed that God told me not to go back to Herod. In my dream God told me that Herod is a wicked man. He wants to kill the new King."

"I had the same dream!" exclaimed another.

"I did too!" said a third.

"God must have told us this so that Jesus would be kept safe," they all agreed. "We must go back home another way."

The wise men turned their caravan away from Jerusalem. As they rode through the desert, they praised God for sending His Son.

"I am glad we gave our gifts to Jesus," said one wise man, "for Jesus is God's special gift to us."

"We gave our best," the others agreed. "But it was so little compared to God's gift—the very best treasure of all!"

Gold, Frankincense, and Myrrh

Eileen M. Berry

Gold

Gold is a bright yellow metal. It is one of the best metals because it is beautiful and hard to find, and it does not rust. Gold lasts for a long time. Because all of these good things are true of gold, its price is very high.

Miner's pan of gold

Most people think that gold is only in the ground. But gold can also be found in water. Pure gold is heavy, but it is very soft and easy to bend. Before gold can be made into coins or jewelry, it has to be mixed with harder metals like copper, silver, or zinc.

Kings in the past have owned many things made of gold. The wise men chose well when they gave gold as a gift to Jesus. Gold is fit for kings, and Jesus Christ is King of kings.

Frankincense

Frankincense is a sticky matter, much like sap. It comes from trees in Somalia and Saudi Arabia. Pale yellow drops of frankincense, called tears, can be melted into oil. The oil has a spicy smell, and people use it to make perfumes.

Many years ago, people used frankincense as *incense*. Incense is any oil or powder that is burned for its sweet odor. It was used to worship God. The wise men's gift of frankincense was very fitting for Jesus. He is the only true God, and one day everyone will worship Him.

Myrrh

Myrrh is also a saplike matter from trees. The trees that myrrh comes from grow in Saudi Arabia and Ethiopia. Like frankincense, myrrh is used in perfumes. Heating myrrh and then cooling it turns it into an oil. Sometimes people burn myrrh just to let it give off its sweet smell.

Myrrh is used to make bodies ready for burial. When the wise men gave myrrh to the Lord Jesus, they made a good choice. One day this King would die for our sin. He would be buried, and He would rise from the dead.

The wise men gave Jesus their finest gifts. The finest gift you can give to Jesus is not gold or frankincense or myrrh. It is your heart.

Johann Boeckhorst, detail from Adoration of the Magi, *The Bob Jones University Collection*

Squirrel's Treasure

Becky Davis / illustrated by Stephanie True

I Want a Treasure

The sun shone brightly in the forest. Beaver felt the cool breeze blowing through his window. He hummed a happy tune as he wrapped a scarf around his neck. Off he went to visit his good friend Squirrel.

Rap! Rap! Rap! Beaver's tail knocked sharply against the wall. A gloomy voice called, "Come in." When Beaver went in, he saw Squirrel sitting at the table with his chin in his hands.

"Why are you sad, Squirrel?" asked Beaver.

Squirrel stood up and walked slowly across the room. "I want to find a precious treasure," he said. "I won't be happy until I have a treasure as good as the ones in this book." He held a large book with many pictures.

Beaver looked carefully at the book. There were chests filled with gold and silver. There were rings and bracelets of diamonds. There were treasures of all kinds.

Beaver scratched his head. "How can you get a treasure?" he asked. "No one in the forest has enough money for such grand things."

288

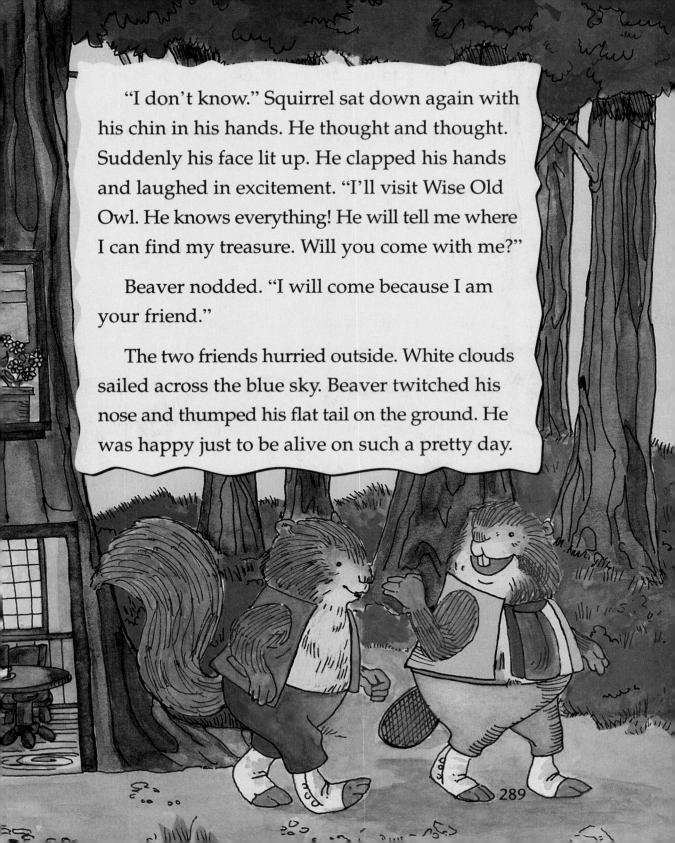

"I don't know." Squirrel sat down again with his chin in his hands. He thought and thought. Suddenly his face lit up. He clapped his hands and laughed in excitement. "I'll visit Wise Old Owl. He knows everything! He will tell me where I can find my treasure. Will you come with me?"

Beaver nodded. "I will come because I am your friend."

The two friends hurried outside. White clouds sailed across the blue sky. Beaver twitched his nose and thumped his flat tail on the ground. He was happy just to be alive on such a pretty day.

289

But Squirrel did not think about the blue sky or the white clouds. All he could think about was his treasure. In fact, he thought about it so hard that he did not look where he was going. At the edge of the brook, Squirrel's foot slipped on a wet stone. With a splash, he fell into the cold water.

"Help me! Help me!" He waved his arms wildly as he called. "I can't swim. Please pull me out!"

Beaver hurried to the brook and jumped in. In no time at all he had pulled Squirrel to the other side of the brook.

Squirrel shivered and shook from head to foot. "I'm cold and wet," he said. "But thank you for pulling me out of the water. You're a good friend."

Look in the Pond

At last the two friends stood underneath Owl's tree and looked up. Wise Old Owl stared back at them, not moving or even blinking his eyes.

Squirrel twisted his paws together and scuffed his toe in the dirt. Wise Old Owl looked so stern! At last Squirrel cleared his throat and began.

"Wise Old Owl," Squirrel said, "I want to find a precious treasure. I want to be rich. You know so much, and you are a wise owl. Will you tell me where I can find a special treasure?"

Owl's eyes blinked once. "Look in the pond," he said. That was all. He ruffled his feathers, and then he closed his eyes.

When Squirrel heard these words, his little ears twitched and his eyes became bright. "In the pond! In the pond!" he said. "We can't waste a moment, Beaver! There must be gold in the pond!"

Squirrel started running toward the pond. Beaver was not so fast. He had a hard time keeping up with Squirrel. But once again, Squirrel did not look where he was going. He caught his foot between two tree roots.

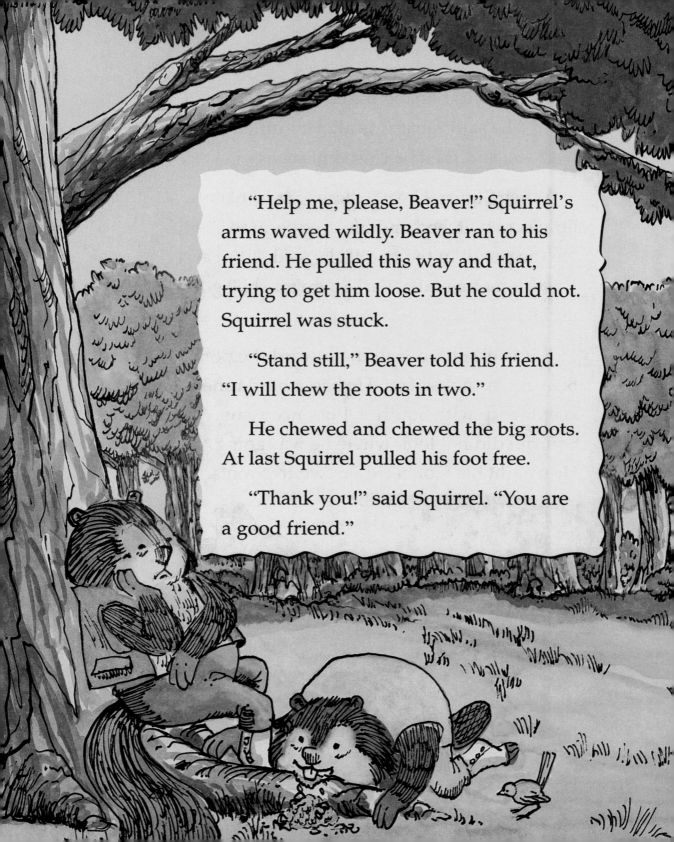

"Help me, please, Beaver!" Squirrel's arms waved wildly. Beaver ran to his friend. He pulled this way and that, trying to get him loose. But he could not. Squirrel was stuck.

"Stand still," Beaver told his friend. "I will chew the roots in two."

He chewed and chewed the big roots. At last Squirrel pulled his foot free.

"Thank you!" said Squirrel. "You are a good friend."

The Rock in the Pond

Beaver and Squirrel walked the rest of the way to the pond. They stood at the edge and looked in. The water was as smooth and as clear as glass.

"All I can see is you and me," Squirrel said with surprise. "Maybe there is something on the bottom of the pond that we should see. Will you go down and look?"

"Yes, I'll look," said Beaver, and he jumped into the cold water.

In a few moments Beaver's head popped back up. His teeth held a bright rock. Many different colors sparkled in the sunlight.

Beaver carefully laid the rock in front of his friend. "Maybe this is your treasure," he said.

"Yes, this must be it," Squirrel said. He grabbed the rock and turned it this way and that. He quivered all over with happiness. "Now we can go home."

That night Squirrel put the rock next to his pillow. He dreamed of all the things he would be able to do with his new treasure.

The sun rose bright and red the next morning. Squirrel sat up and stretched. Then he quickly reached for his rock.

It wasn't bright and sparkling anymore! It was dry and dark and ugly. "This rock isn't a real treasure after all," Squirrel cried. "When it's dry, it doesn't even sparkle."

He hurried over to Beaver's house and went
in without knocking. "You must come with me
back to Owl's tree," he said. "I have to speak to
him again."

Through the woods and over the brook
the two friends hurried together. When they
reached Owl's tree, they found him staring
straight at them. He was not moving a feather
or blinking an eye.

Squirrel stood uneasily on one foot.
Then he stood on the other. "Wise Old
Owl," he said, "you told me to look in
the pond for my treasure, and I did.
I found a rock that I thought was my
treasure, but it was not a real treasure.
Today it is dry and dark and ugly.
What should I do now?"

Owl's head moved a little, and
his eyes blinked twice. "Look in the
pond," he said. He would not say
another word. He ruffled his feathers
a little, and then he closed his eyes.

Finding the Treasure

"Look in the pond. Look in the pond," Squirrel muttered as he walked away.

Beaver ran after him. "Maybe there is still a treasure there that we missed," he said.

Squirrel's face brightened. "At least we could look." So the two friends hurried back to the pond.

Together they tiptoed up to the pond and stood at the edge looking in. The water was as smooth and as clear as glass.

"All you can see is you and me," said Squirrel. "I think Owl must be wrong."

"But maybe we are supposed to wait," said Beaver. "Maybe the treasure will come to you."

So the two friends sat down on the ground. They stared into the water and waited.

As Squirrel stared into the water at himself and his good friend, he began to remember all the things Beaver had done. He remembered how Beaver had come on this treasure hunt without grumbling. He remembered how Beaver had saved him from drowning in the brook. He remembered how Beaver had freed him from the tree roots when he was stuck. He remembered how Beaver had dived into the cold water of the pond to look for the treasure for him.

"What a good friend Beaver is," he thought to himself.

Suddenly Squirrel jumped up from the ground and hopped around and around. His tail twitched and his whiskers wiggled. "I have found it!" he cried. "Owl was right! I looked and looked into the pond, and I found treasure. See!" He pulled Beaver over to the edge of the pond.

"Look in the water. A good friend is the great treasure! I must thank Owl."

Beaver was happy Squirrel had found a treasure, but he asked, "Does that mean you won't be rich?"

"Oh, but I am very rich!" replied Squirrel. "Anyone is rich enough who has a friend as faithful as you. Will you come with me to see Owl?"

"I would be glad to," Beaver said. And the two set off together to thank the Wise Old Owl.

Glossary

This glossary has information about selected words found in this reader. You can find meanings of words as they are used in the stories. Certain unusual words such as foreign names are included so that you can pronounce them correctly when you read.

The pronunciation symbols below show how to pronounce each vowel and several of the less familiar consonants.

ă	pat	ĕ	pet	îr	fierce
ā	pay	ē	be	ŏ	pot
âr	care	ĭ	pit	ō	go
ä	father	ī	pie	ô	paw, for, ball

oi	oil	ŭ	cut	zh	vision
o͝o	book	ûr	fur	ə	ago, item,
o͞o	boot	*th*	the		pencil, atom,
yo͞o	abuse	th	thin		circus
ou	out	hw	which	ər	butter

A **a • bil • i • ty** | ə **bĭl´** ĭ tē | The power or skill to do something.

antenna

a • lert | ə **lûrt´** | Quick to notice or understand.

al • ler • gies | **ăl´** ər jēz | Unpleasant physical reactions to certain foods, pollens, furs, animals, or other things.

amen | **ā´ mĕn´** | or | **ä´ mĕn´** | A word that means "so be it" or "truly." **Amen** is often said at the end of a prayer. It is also said at the end of a statement with which one agrees.

an • ten • na | ăn **tĕn´** ə | Plural *antennae*. One of a pair of long, thin feelers on the head of some animals. Insects, lobsters, and shrimp have antennae.

Australia

a • part • ment | ə **pärt´** mənt | A room or set of rooms for one household. An apartment is in a building or house that usually has other rooms or sets of rooms like it.

ap • peared | ə **pîrd´** | Came into view; was seen.

Aus • tra • lia | ô **strāl´** yə | A continent southeast of Asia between the Pacific and Indian Oceans.

B **bleak** | blēk | Without cheer; dreary.

both • ered | **bŏ***th***´** ərd | Gave trouble to; annoyed.

brass | brăs | A yellowish metal that contains copper and zinc.

buggy

bug • gy | **bŭg´** ē | A small, light carriage pulled by a horse.

cap • tain | kăp´ tən | The leader of a group.

car • a • van | kăr´ ə văn | A group of people, animals, or vehicles traveling together, usually in a long line.

ce • dar | sē´ dər | An evergreen tree with reddish wood that has a pleasant smell. Cedars are related to pines and firs.

cedar

ă	pat	ĕ	pet
ā	pay	ē	be
âr	care	ĭ	pit
ä	father	ī	pie
îr	fierce	oi	oil
ŏ	pot	o͝o	book
ō	go	o͞o	boot
ô	paw,	yo͞o	abuse
	for	ou	out
ŭ	cut	ə	ago,
ûr	fur		item,
th	the		pencil,
th	thin		atom,
hw	which		circus
zh	vision	ər	butter

chat • ter | chăt´ ər | To make quick, rattling noises.

chick • a • dee | chĭk´ ə dē´ | A small, plump bird with gray, black, and white feathers. It has a call that sounds like its name.

chore | chôr | or | chōr | A small job, usually done on a regular schedule.

Chris • tian | krĭs´ chən | One who has accepted Jesus Christ as Savior.

cit • i • zen | sĭt´ ĭ zən | Someone who is a member of a country, either by being born there or by choosing to become a member. A citizen has certain rights from his country and also some responsibilities.

clev • er | klĕv´ ər | Having a quick mind; smart; bright.

cliff

cliff | klĭf | A high, steep, or overhanging face of earth or rock.

clump | klŭmp | A thick group of trees or bushes.

coil | koil | To wind around a number of times.

clump

col • o • ny | **kŏl´** ə nē | A group of the same kind of animals or plants living closely together.

colony

com • rade | **kŏm´** răd | A companion who shares one's activities.

crab • grass | **krăb´** grăs´ | A bothersome lawn weed common throughout North America. Common characteristics of crabgrass include its thick, low-growing stems and coarse leaves.

crack • led | **krăk´** əld | Past tense and past participle of **crackle**: To make slight, sharp, snapping sounds.

crabgrass

croc • o • dile | **krŏk´** ə dīl´ | A large reptile with thick skin, sharp teeth, and long, narrow jaws. Crocodiles live in wet places throughout the Tropics.

crouch | krouch | To bend low; stoop; squat.

D **dan • dy** | **dăn´** dē | Something very good of its kind.

dis • a • bil • i • ties | **dĭs´** ə **bĭl´** ĭ tēz | Plural for **disability**: A physical or mental condition that hinders one from performing one or more physical or mental functions.

dish • cloth | **dĭsh´** klôth | or | **dĭsh´** klŏth | A cloth used to wash dishes.

dread • ed | **drĕd´** ĭd | Greatly feared.

crocodile **E** **ea • ger** | **ē´** gər | Wanting something very much; full of desire.

e • lec • tric • i • ty | ĭ lĕk **trĭs´** ĭ tē | A form of energy that can be sent through wires in a flow of tiny particles. Electricity is used to produce light and heat and to run motors.

el • e • phant | **ĕl´** ə fənt | A very large animal of Africa or Asia; it has long tusks and a long trunk.

elephant

Eli | **ē´** lī | A biblical character; the priest who taught Samuel.

eu • ca • lyp • tus | yo͞o´ kə **lĭp´** təs | A tall tree that grows in Australia and other warm regions. An oil with a strong smell is made from its leaves. Its wood is used for building.

eucalyptus

ex • claim | ik **sklām´** | To speak out suddenly and loudly, as from surprise.

F   **faint** | fānt | Not clearly heard, weak: *a faint cry.*

field • er | **fēl´** dər | A baseball player who has a position out in the field.

fin • gers | **fĭng´** gərs | The plural form of **finger**: any one of the five body parts that extends outward from the hand.

ă	pat	ĕ	pet
ā	pay	ē	be
âr	care	ĭ	pit
ä	father	ī	pie
îr	fierce	oi	oil
ŏ	pot	o͝o	book
ō	go	o͞o	boot
ô	paw,	yo͞o	abuse
	for	ou	out
ŭ	cut	ə	ago,
ûr	fur		item,
th	the		pencil,
th	thin		atom,
hw	which		circus
zh	vision	ər	butter

flock | flŏk | A group of one kind of animal that lives, travels, or feeds together.

frank • in • cense | **frăngk´** ĭn sĕns´ | A sweet-smelling incense.

G   **gem** | jĕm | A precious stone that has been cut and polished to be used as a jewel.

gem

gloves

gen • er • ous | jĕn´ ər əs | Unselfish.

glare | glâr | To stare angrily.

glo • ri • ous | glôr´ ē əs | or | glōr´ ē əs |
Magnificent.

gloves | glŭvz | Plural of **glove**: A covering for the
hand with a separate section for each finger and the
thumb.

H **haz • ard •ous** | hăz´ ər dəs | Characterized by
danger.

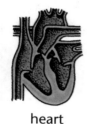

heart

heart | härt | The organ that pumps blood
throughout the body.

hon • ey | hŭn´ ē | A thick, sweet, yellowish
substance made by bees. It is made from nectar that
the bees gather from flowers. Honey is good to eat.

hor • ri • ble | hôr´ ə bəl | Causing horror; terrible.

I **im • por • tant** | īm pôr´ tnt | Having great value,
meaning, or influence; significant.

J **Je • sus** | jē´ zəs | The human name of the Son of
God, who came to this world to save people from
their sins, as the Bible tells us. He is also called Jesus
Christ or Christ.

honey

K **kan • ga • roo** | kăng gə rōō´ | An animal of
Australia with long, strong hind legs and a long tail.
The female carries her newborn young in a pouch
on the outside of her body.

king • dom | kĭng´ dəm | A country that is ruled by a king or queen.

ko • a • la | kō ä´ lə | An animal of Australia that looks something like a small, furry teddy bear. It lives in eucalyptus trees and feeds on their leaves.

leaves

L **leaves** | lēvz | Plural of **leaf**: A thin, flat, green part that grows from the stem of a plant.

lis • ten | lĭs´ ən | To try to hear something.

liz • ard | lĭz´ ərd | An animal that has a scaly body, four legs, and a long tail. There are many kinds of lizards. Most of them live in warm parts of the world.

lizard

M **mar • vel • ous** | mär´ və ləs | Causing wonder or great admiration; amazing.

mis • sion • ar • y | mĭsh´ ə nĕr´ ē | A person sent out to spread the gospel of salvation to the world.

mouth | mouth | 1. The part of the body through which a person or animal takes in food. 2. An opening.

moun • tain li • on | moun´ tən lī´ ən | A large light-brown wildcat of western North America and South America. Also called *cougar* or *puma*.

myrrh | mûr | A sweet-smelling perfume of the Far East, used as incense.

N **New Test • a • ment** | noo tĕs´ tə mənt | The second part of the Bible; the 27 books beginning with the Gospel of Matthew and ending with the book of Revelation.

ă	pat	ĕ	pet
ā	pay	ē	be
âr	care	ĭ	pit
ä	father	ī	pie
îr	fierce	oi	oil
ŏ	pot	͞o͞o	book
ō	go	͞o͞o	boot
ô	paw,	y͞o͞o	abuse
	for	ou	out
ŭ	cut	ə	ago,
ûr	fur		item,
th	the		pencil,
th	thin		atom,
hw	which		circus
zh	vision	ər	butter

mountain lion

P   **pack** | păk | A group of similar animals.

pal • ace | păl´ ĭs | The official residence of a king, queen, or other ruler.

palace

par • don me | pär´ dn mē | A courteous expression used in asking someone to excuse one's actions.

pas • sen • ger | păs´ ən jər | A person riding in a train, airplane, bus, ship, car, or other vehicle.

pitch • er | pĭch´ ər | 1. The baseball player who throws the ball to the batter. 2. A container used to hold and pour out liquids. A pitcher has a handle on one side and a spout on the other.

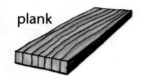

pitcher

plank

plank | plăngk | A thick, wide, long piece of wood that has been sawed.

plod | plŏd | To walk heavily or with great effort.

pre • cious | prĕsh´ əs | Of high price or value.

pre • dic • a • ment | prĭ dĭk´ ə mənt | A situation, usually a difficult one, for which the solution requires some thought.

pre • tend • ed | prĭ tĕnd´ əd | Past tense and past participle of **pretend:** To make believe.

pro • tect | prə tĕkt´ | To keep from harm; guard; preserve.

pun • ish | pŭn´ ĭsh | To make someone suffer or pay a penalty for a crime, fault, or misbehavior.

ă	pat	ĕ	pet
ā	pay	ē	be
âr	care	ĭ	pit
ä	father	ī	pie
îr	fierce	oi	oil
ŏ	pot	ŏŏ	book
ō	go	ŏŏ	boot
ô	paw,	yŏŏ	abuse
	for	ou	out
ŭ	cut	ə	ago,
ûr	fur		item,
th	the		pencil,
th	thin		atom,
hw	which		circus
zh	vision	ər	butter

310

py • thon | **pī´** thŏn | A very large, nonpoisonous snake of Africa, Asia, and Australia. Pythons coil around and crush the animals they eat.

python

Q **quiv • er** | **kwĭv´** ər | To shake with a slight vibrating motion.

R **rash** | rǎsh | An outbreak of little red spots on the skin. A rash usually itches.

re • mem • ber | rĭ **mĕm´** bər | To keep carefully in one's memory.

rob • ber | **rŏb´** ər | A person who robs; a thief.

ruf • fle | **rŭf´** əl | To disturb the smooth appearance of.

scribe

S **scarf** | skärf | A piece of cloth worn around the neck or head for warmth or decoration.

scribe | skrīb | A person who copied books, letters, and other kinds of written material before printing was invented.

scroll | skrōl | A roll of paper, parchment, or other material that has writing on it. Each end is rolled around a rod or cylinder.

scroll

scuff | skŭf | To scrape or drag the feet in walking.

shad • ow | **shǎd´** ō | A dark area where some or all of the light is blocked by someone or something.

shell | shĕl | 1. A hard outer covering of certain animals or plants. Crabs, lobsters, turtles, eggs, and nuts have shells. 2. To remove the outer covering from.

shepherd

silver

soldier ant

ă	pat	ĕ	pet
ā	pay	ē	be
âr	care	ĭ	pit
ä	father	ī	pie
îr	fierce	oi	oil
ŏ	pot	ŏŏ	book
ō	go	ōō	boot
ô	paw,	yōō	abuse
	for	ou	out
ŭ	cut	ə	ago,
ûr	fur		item,
th	the		pencil,
th	thin		atom,
hw	which		circus
zh	vision	ər	butter

shep • herd | **shĕp´** ərd | A person who takes care of a flock of sheep.

shiv • ered | **shĭv´** ərd | The past tense of **shiver:** To shake or tremble from cold, fear, or excitement in a way one cannot control.

sil • ver | **sĭl´** vər | A soft, shiny grayish metal. Silver is used to make money and jewelry. Silver is one of the chemical elements.

slith • ered | **slĭth´** ərd | Past tense of **slither:** To move along by gliding as a snake.

snarl | snärl | To growl, especially while showing teeth.

snatch | snătch | To grab suddenly and quickly.

sol • dier ant | **sōl´** jər ănt | An ant that is characterized by a large head and powerful jaws. In some species of ants, the soldier ant's main function is to protect the colony from danger.

son | sŭn | A male child.

sor • ry | **sŏr´** ē | or | **sôr´** ē | Feeling or expression of sadness, sympathy, or regret.

spark • le | **spär´** kəl | To give off sparks of light; glitter.

spe • cial | **spĕsh´** əl | Different from what is usual or common; exceptional.

spring | sprĭng | A natural fountain or flow of water.

312

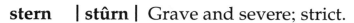

squir • rel | skwûr′ əl | or | skwĭr′ əl | An animal with gray or reddish-brown fur and a bushy tail.

squirrel

staff | stăf | or | stäf | A long stick with a hook at one end; used by a shepherd.

stern | stûrn | Grave and severe; strict.

stray | strā | Wandering; lost.

street • car | strēt′ kär′ | A car that runs on rails and carries passengers along a regular route through city streets.

sway | swā | To move from side to side.

T   **tab • er • na • cle** | tăb′ ər năk′ əl | A temple or place of worship.

streetcar

tas • sel | tăs′ əl | A bunch of loose threads on cords that are tied together at one end and hanging free at the other.

taught | tôt | Past tense and past participle of **teach:** to help someone learn; give knowledge of or lessons in.

thrust | thrŭst | To push with force; shove.

thun • der | thŭn′ dər | To produce sounds like the rumbling or crashing noise that accompanies a bolt of lightning.

tongue | tŭng | A muscular piece of flesh in the mouth. The tongue is used in tasting and helps in chewing and swallowing food. People also use their tongues for talking.

tassel

valley

wolf

train • er | **trā´** nər | A person who trains a person or animal, especially one who coaches athletes, race horses, or show animals.

trem • ble | **trĕm´** bəl | To shake, as from cold or fear; shiver.

trot | trŏt | To run quickly.

twitch | twĭch | To move with a quick jerk.

V **val • ley** | **văl´** ē | A long, narrow area of low land between mountains or hills.

vel • vet | **vĕl´** vĭt | A soft, smooth cloth with a short, thick, plush surface.

W **warts** | wôrtz | Plural of **wart:** A small, hard lump that grows on the skin. It is caused by a virus.

whis • pered | **hwĭs´** pərd | or | **wĭs´** pərd | Past tense and past participle of **whisper:** To speak or say very softly.

wob • ble | **wŏb´** əl | To move or cause to move unsteadily from side to side.

wolf | woolf | An animal that lives mostly in northern regions and feeds on the flesh of other animals.

wor • ship | **wûr´** shĭp | To love and obey God from the heart.

Z **ze • bra** | **zē´** brə | An African animal that is related to the horse. Its body is marked with black or brown and white stripes.

ă	pat	ĕ	pet
ā	pay	ē	be
âr	care	ĭ	pit
ä	father	ī	pie
îr	fierce	oi	oil
ŏ	pot	oo	book
ō	go	oo	boot
ô	paw,	yoo	abuse
	for	ou	out
ŭ	cut	ə	ago,
ûr	fur		item,
th	the		pencil,
th	thin		atom,
hw	which		circus
zh	vision	ər	butter

zebra

The Boy Who Cried "Wolf"

Morgan Reed Persun

A play is one way to make a fable seem more like real life. This play happens in two different places. Some folks get ready for a fair in the village. At the same time, a shepherd is watching his sheep on the hill. Choose places in your room for both settings. Make props and costumes from materials you can easily find in class or at home. Think about what the shepherd boy learns as you put on the play.

Cast

Shepherd

Villager 1

Villager 2

Villager 3

Wolf/Jacob (Villager 4)

3 Sheep

Villager 1: Hurry with the paint, Jacob!

Villager 2: Any more flowers for the wreaths?

Villager 3: All the streets need sweeping again.

Shepherd: Look at them down there, getting ready for the fair, all the flags and games. And here I am up here all alone. It isn't fair!

Sheep: Baa, baa—Baa, baa.

Shepherd: I know—I know what will get me some company and quick!

WOLF! WOLF! HELP, WOLF!

Villager 1: The shepherd boy! Quick! *(They all drop their work and run.)*

Villager 2: Well, where is the wolf? *(As they arrive, they look around for the wolf.)*

Villager 3: Which way did he go? *(The boy looks guilty.)*

Villager 4: There is no wolf, is there, boy?

Shepherd: Well, not really.

Villager 1 *(scowling at him)***:** That wasn't smart. Don't play that trick again, you hear?

Shepherd *(watching the villagers leave)***:** They didn't stay long, did they?

Sheep: Baa, baa—Baa, baa.

Shepherd: And I don't think it was such a bad thing I did. They don't have so very far to come, after all. All they're doing is getting ready for the fair. I'm going to get them to come up here again.
WOLF! WOLF! HELP, WOLF!

Villager 2 *(pausing)*: We ought to see about it, really. It might be real this time. *(They run, but not as fast this time.)*

Shepherd: I'm delighted that you came back.

Villager 4: Where is the wolf? Is there really a wolf here?

Shepherd: No—I just wanted some company up here. Everyone is having fun without me!

Villager 3: We all have our jobs to do! Now you do yours and no more of this foolishness! *(They leave, shaking their heads and frowning. Villager 4 goes offstage to put on wolf costume.)*

Shepherd: Easy for them to talk! They all have

each other to work with. I have to stay up here by myself. Look at them down there, talking to each other.

Sheep: Baa, baa—Baa, baa.

Shepherd: I think I should be allowed some company that says something besides "Baa" all the time.

(*Wolf appears far behind the shepherd.*)

What possible difference could it make to them to come up here for an hour or two to visit?

Sheep: Baa, baa—Baa, baa.

(*Wolf creeps slowly toward the shepherd.*)

I think they ought to think of how lonely I am with only woolly friends.

(*Wolf leaps in front of the shepherd.*)

WOLF! HELP! WOLF! HELP! HELP!

Villager 1 (*looking up casually*)**:** There he goes again. Some boys never learn.

Villager 2: I have made too many trips up that

hill for nothing today. I am not going up again!

Shepherd (*with great fear*): HELP!

Wolf: Nobody is going to come now, boy.

Shepherd: Yes, they are! HELP! WOLF!

Wolf: I've been watching you, boy. You finished your chances of getting any help that last time you called the whole town up here for no reason. I've got you now.

Shepherd: What are you going to do?

Wolf: Well, I was going to eat up the sheep.

Sheep: Baa, baa—Baa, baa.

Wolf: But, to tell the truth, I feel sorry for them, having such a selfish shepherd as you. Maybe I'll eat *you* instead.

Shepherd: Oh, please don't eat me. Please!

Wolf: I would be doing the town a favor, I think.

(*He removes the wolf costume to show he is a villager in disguise.*)

Shepherd: Why—why! you're Jacob!

Jacob: So, I am. And I hope you are a wiser shepherd boy than you were before!

Shepherd: I promise NEVER to cry "wolf" again just to get company.

Jacob: That's good. I think I'll see about getting another boy to help you tend the sheep.

Shepherd: Would you? Oh, thank you! That would be grand!

(The two shake hands, and Jacob goes back to town.)

Sheep: Baa, baa—Baa, baa.

Shepherd *(to sheep)*: You know, my woolly friends, you are not such bad company after all.